D1324015

FOR MY PARENTS
KARIN AND OTTO
BREKKE

SALLY ANN

– POVERTY TO HOPE

BO BREKKE | KNUT BRY

SALLY ANN ®

Shield Books

© **The Salvation Army United Kingdom and Ireland Territory 2005**

Photographer: Knut Bry

page 6 and back cover: Rupert Sieger, portraits Birgitte and Bo Brekke

page 8: Robin Bryant, portrait Brian Turner

page 9, 96, 103, 104, 134: Nina Jernberg *(9: Upper right, 103: Bottom left, 104: Left, 134: Right)*

page 11: Jan Aasmann Størksen, Jens Barland and Nina Jernberg

page 61: Elisabeth Tollisen, photo Sally Ann shop

page 61, 113, 125: Marius Tharaldsen, photo Sally Ann products

page 103: The Salvation Army Bangladesh *(bottom right)*

page 113, 152: Jan Aasmann Størksen

Designed by: Uniform, Norway

Publisher: The Salvation Army United Kingdom and Ireland Territory

ISBN: 0-85412-736-4

All rights reserved.

Under no circumstances can any part of this book be reproduced or copied
in any form without the prior permission of the copyright owners.

SALLY ANN

– POVERTY TO HOPE

BO BREKKE | KNUT BRY

CONTENTS

Bo Brekke was born in Norway, but from the age of 10 he spent 9 years with his parents in Switzerland and Germany before returning to study at Jeløy Folk High School. In 1978 Bo met Birgitte Nielsen – a Danish nurse – as they waited for interview at the start of Salvation Army officer-training in London. It was 'love at first sight' and two years later, now married, Bo and Birgitte were appointed as officers in Norway. Bo felt called to serve overseas, but not until 1986 did Birgitte feel God calling her to service in Asia. After that, six years in Sri Lanka were followed by seven years in Bangladesh where their passion for Fairtrade found expression. In 2002 they became divisional leaders in North Scotland and are currently appointed to Moscow to serve in the Eastern Europe Territory of The Salvation Army. They have two sons and one granddaughter.

My wife Birgitte and I were privileged to serve in Bangladesh for seven years, from 1995 to 2002. That, together with our more than six years in Sri Lanka, has enriched our lives beyond description. It has changed our views on almost all issues. South Asia has been a 'learning ground' for us. Here we have been confronted with the harsh realities of life as faced by a majority of the world's population – and we have been challenged in our understanding of poverty and what we should do about it. We have come to see that the gospel message is the one thing that elevates the mission organisation from the ranks of development agencies and positions us uniquely to deal with the problems of poverty.

The events about to be told are proof of the gospel at work. They are an account of meaningful mission to the poor. 'We' tell the story. The 'we' are Birgitte and me. The story is told from our perspective. It is a true account, but it is subjective. Any interpretation of events or any inaccuracies are our responsibility.

The story is about people. That extraordinary and wonderful group of officers and employees, soldiers and friends who make up The Salvation Army in Bangladesh. We have never met a group of people with a more positive and willing spirit. They are prepared to try anything for the Lord. It is about people in the towns and villages of Bangladesh. The people of Bangladesh have a remarkable capacity for adapting to seemingly impossible circumstances and they cope with difficulties in a way and with a stoicism that is lost in the West. We admire them.

Birgitte deserves special mention. Though I have done the actual writing, Birgitte's input to the book has been immense. Every line of every chapter has been discussed with her. Without her, *Sally Ann* would never have happened. She took hold of the fledgling idea and nurtured it through its infancy. She was designer and producer, shop manager and instructor and she undertook any other role that was needed. Nothing – however good an idea it is – will become reality without hard work.

Bo Brekke · Aberdeen, January 2005

Sometimes we look at the world, the problems seem so big, that we feel helpless, as if there's nothing we can do. This begs the question – what *can* we do about the millions of people around the world struggling to survive on less than a dollar a day?

This is why fair trade is so exciting and why it is capturing the imagination of consumers in the UK and across the developed world. Simply by changing our buying habits we can directly benefit producers and workers in developing countries and ensure that they receive a fair price for their goods.

The story of The Salvation Army's Sally Ann Fairtrade project, pioneered in Bangladesh, is thoroughly uplifting. It shows that with a lot of vision and perseverance people can be empowered to improve their own lives. I've known The Salvation Army throughout most of my life and I can see that fair trade and The Salvation Army are perfect for each other. Engaging in fair trade means The Salvation Army can help people to help themselves, providing a secure and stable future for them and their families. It's The Salvation Army's mission, driven by its Christian belief, in a nutshell.

Fair trade is about us all. It's not about doing special things – it's about building fairness into the fabric of our everyday lives in the way that we shop. I hope this book will encourage everyone to think about the people who cultivate our food or produce our handicrafts. So next time you get the opportunity, go on - use the fair trade option. It won't cost that much more but you can be assured that more of your money is going to the people who have worked so hard to produce whatever it is that you are buying.

As for the quality of some of the fair trade food you can buy – well, it's fantastic. Believe me, on that score I really know what I'm talking about!

Brian Turner, CBE · London, January 2005

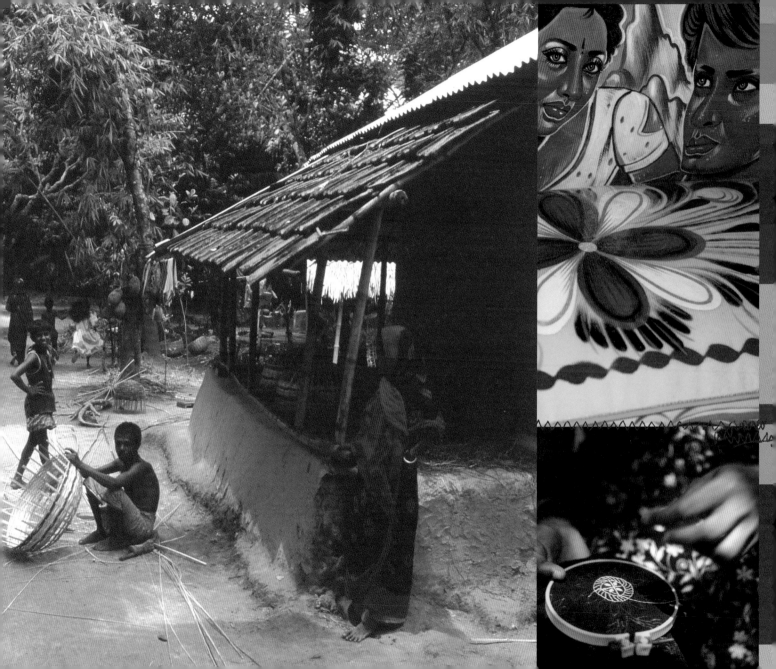

Sally Ann Norway. Bangladesh. Kenya, fair trade and empowering of the poor.

Sally Ann, impacting the life of people

'**If this man William Booth** hadn't already lived his life, I am sure the Almighty would have let him be born in Bangladesh.' Our Muslim neighbour looked up from the book we had given him to read. 'We need this kind of person who will not only talk about religion, but do religion.' The story about to be told is the story of William and Catherine Booth's vision come true in Bangladesh. For the uninitiated reader: William and Catherine Booth lived in England in the 19th century. Out of sheer frustration with established religion, they developed The Salvation Army to reach the poor with a gospel of salvation and practical care.

Booth published his dream for a better world in 1890, in the book *In Darkest England and the Way Out*. An important part of the 'way out', as he saw it, was to provide work for the poor who had already been helped with food and shelter. The Salvation Army opened England's first employment exchange. The Salvation Army established a match factory to combat the scandal of workers suffering from phosphorous poisoning. The Salvation Army started farms to train men in agriculture. It even went into the life assurance business to help people at the very sensitive time of bereavement, creating many worthwhile jobs in the process. A popular Salvation Army ballad of the time ran:

> *Oh, the General's dream, that noble scheme,*
> *Gives John Jones work to do;*
> *He'll have a bed and be well fed,*
> *When the General's dream comes true.*

Sally Ann is a continuation of Booth's story. *Sally Ann* is about putting bread on people's table. It is about empowerment of the poor. It is about fair trade. It is about a 'way out' that is entirely in line with the gospel of Jesus.

Sally Ann is an unfinished story. It started in Bangladesh. It has spread to Norway. Links have been established with Kenya and Tanzania. It will soon be on all continents, in every country where The Salvation Army is at work. That is the vision.

In the Jessore
brothel: Josef Das
and Salvationist
workers.

Producing tin cards
for Sally Ann

In Salvation Army projects, women have always been a target group.

Sixty village women in Jessore looked to The Salvation Army to improve their lives. Their lives were defined by the customs and cultures of the small villages that make up the surroundings of Jessore town. The modern, worldwide phenomenon of urbanisation is rapidly affecting Bangladesh, with millions of people being drawn to the ever-growing cities in search of work. But the vast majority of the population still live in rural communities.

Life goes on much as it has for generations. Life centres on the family homestead, the *bari*, and within it everyone has his or her well-defined role. It isn't necessarily an easy life, but it is a well ordered life and – for most – a good life. Family and community values are important. People care and have time for each other. The pace of life is unhurried. There is time to enjoy the village bard and the dancers. Religious festivals are important highlights. Village life is also a hard life. People work long days to make the fields yield their harvest. Money is scarce for material necessities, let alone for luxuries. Healthcare is often lacking. Education is still for the minority.

The Salvation Army has concentrated its Community Health and Development work in Jessore on 18 rural villages 'allocated' to the organisation by the local government. For years, the Army has been part of village life as the sole provider of healthcare and education. The nature of the work has developed and changed over time. It has moved ever more away from institution-based work to community-based activity. Rather than external experts providing services, emphasis is placed on empowering local people to learn the skills necessary. '*Bari* mothers' – village midwives – monitor expectant mothers and deliver most of the babies at home. Only pregnant women with complications are referred to the clinic. Village health workers visit every family within their home community, checking children's growth, answering the parents' questions, offering advice on family planning. Young people are taught how to test the water in the village wells for arsenic poisoning, a growing and largely unexplained problem in Bangladesh. Community support groups meet regularly with the Salvation Army facilitator to discuss problems and seek solutions. There is still a need for the clinic. The doctors, nurses and lab technicians still have plenty to do. The village primary schools still continue to offer education. But increasingly the Army's role has become one of facilitating capacity development within people. It speaks well for the quality of the Army's work that all the key indicators used to measure the population's health and educational standards are well on the plus side compared to the national average.

A subtle shift with far-reaching consequences has been the changing role of women in rural Bangladesh in recent years. More girls than ever receive an education. Women become economically active. Women learn of their rights as equal citizens and claim those rights.

In the Army's projects women have been a special target group from the beginning. Adult literacy classes have offered village women the chance to learn to read and write. Various skills-training programmes have led to the commencement of income-generating activities. Women have organised themselves in savings and loan groups. In recent years, women's rights groups have given women legal advice and spoken out against early marriages. It is all part of a social evolution that cannot and should not be halted.

Sixty village women had enrolled in the Army's sewing project in Jessore. They met in small groups and produced embroidered cushion covers, napkins and tablecloths. Traditional techniques and patterns were refined and the end products were mostly of a high quality. The women were pleased. They were paid per finished piece and they could usually add a handsome sum to their family income at the end of each week. The project had been going for two years. The families had come to depend on the extra income. The women met and produced.

For them it was a fair trade. They worked and they were paid.

However, the project had the basic flaw of most projects: it was unsustainable. It could continue only for as long as there were donor funds available. The problem was that fewer and fewer customers wanted to buy the embroideries the women produced. The market was more than satisfied with traditional *Notchi Katha* embroideries. The shops in Dhaka had no interest in buying more. The cupboards in the Salvation Army project office were bursting with embroidered tablecloths and napkins that were of no interest to anyone.

Donor funds were drying up. The women were told that the orders would have to cease. They could no longer expect to be paid by The Salvation Army. It was difficult for the women from Jessore. True, no one could take their newly learned skills from them, but it would be difficult for them and their families without the regular income they had become used to. The project was dubbed the 'project of the broken needles and broken hopes'. There was disappointment and anger when the embroidery project in Jessore came to an end.

We needed a new approach. We needed a sustainable employment project, a model that would not have to depend on external funding. The basic flaw of the 'broken needle project' was that the end product was not marketable. We could not compete in the market for traditional embroideries. The solution was logical and easy: we needed to identify products for which there would be a demand and then teach the women in Jessore how to produce these.

Some simple market research was carried out in Dhaka. All the different shops that sold handicrafts and designer goods were visited. What could one not find there? We read and looked in interior design magazines to discover trends. It was not long before we were able to send the first new design to Jessore. We ordered six place mats: all to have the same modern design, all to be of the same size and colour.

The reasoning behind the new approach had been discussed with the project staff in Jessore. They in turn had explained the need for change to the women. But change does not come easily. The women did not necessarily understand why the traditional patterns would not sell and they most certainly did not like the new ones. We waited a long time for the six sample place mats from Jessore! Finally, they did arrive. There was excitement as the packet was opened. We had great hopes that we had found a new and more sustainable approach. To us, the six place mats were the first concrete proof of a great idea with the potential to help many women in Bangladesh to a regular income.

Excitement turned to disappointment. The place mats before us were of six different sizes. No two of them had the design placed in the same place. The colour of the thread was different on all six. There was clearly a long way to go! The six place mats from Jessore were the real beginning of *Sally Ann* Products. We sent them back and asked the women to start again. We sent the next lot back, too.

The third time they came back in good order. Size, design and colour were all the way we wanted. We paid for them. A principle had been established and we could go on to place more orders. The project of the broken needles taught us valuable lessons. *Sally Ann* would never have started without the failure of the embroidery project in Jessore.

We learned the need to produce for a real market demand. Design, quality control, uniformity of product became key words in our vocabulary. And the village women of Jessore learned the need for change. Market forces had arrived in the villages in Jessore and they would work for the women's benefit.

Salvation Army
farm produce
sold well in Savar
market.

Mark Stanley is a Canadian Salvationist. With his wife Barbara he came on a three-year contract to work for The Salvation Army in Bangladesh. His brief was to look at 'economic development' opportunities for people living within the Army project areas. Mark was well suited for this, being multi-talented and of an entrepreneurial spirit. He would try anything to help people to an income.

In Konejpur he turned the Army garden into a vegetable plot. Lal-shak, a deliciously nutritious, red-leafed vegetable, grew alongside ladies' fingers and pumpkin. The corps also took delivery of a diesel engine that could be used either as an irrigation pump or to power a mechanical plough. Farmers in the village could hire the pump-plough for a modest fee. It worked well for a while. Then the engine broke down and died. It was discovered that the 'Chinese-made' new engine had indeed been assembled from old, discarded engine parts. At least someone had made a good job of that: it had fooled Mark and the entire Salvation Army board that approved the purchase.

In Savar people were sent to the Southern Baptist training farm to learn duck breeding and fish farming. The people who were trained turned the wasteland next to the Savar Girls' Home into a profitable farming operation. Soon, chicken production was added. Eggs and broilers sold well in the local market. After a while the farm in Savar had to give way to the building of a new Salvation Army Training College. More and more people wanted to become Salvation Army officers. The present college in Jessore had long since been outgrown. The location and the land in Savar was ideal for a training centre for the Army in Bangladesh. So Mark's farm had to go.

Mark tried other avenues of economic development. Could Bangladesh maybe benefit from The Salvation Army's worldwide recycling industries? After all, the Army had a 30 per cent share of the international market in recycled clothing.

Could we go into the import business? Could we widen the import to include more than just recycled clothes? What about importing baby nappies? Mark and Barbara had had their first child. They knew how difficult it was to get nappies in the shops of Dhaka. Surely there would be a market? Mark was imaginative. He would let no idea rest without giving it at least a good thought, if not a try. Then his hunger for crisps took hold. Or potato chips, as people on the North American continent would say. After snacking on Bombay sweets and other local delicacies for a while, Mark missed his bag of chips. When he settled in front of the TV at night, the craving became acute. Immediate market research revealed the sad facts: no shop in Dhaka sold potato chips. There was no local variety, and nothing to be found on the shelves with the expensive imported goods.

Mark swung into action. Barbara was ordered out of the kitchen and within an hour he had produced his very first batch of snacks. Not bad at all! This surely could develop into something profitable. The next day Mark had two ladies with him in the kitchen. The resulting product was market-tested in the Salvation Army office. Very acceptable! Production methods were refined, packaging was designed and soon Mark had started to sell the chips to Western people who, like him, were missing the little empty-calorie luxuries from home.

The production moved out of Mark's kitchen. The garage behind the Army Headquarters was turned into a small factory. More workers were hired. Business was good. The American Club, the American International School and some embassies became regular customers.

Mark thought of a name and a logo for his crisps. A silhouette of a Salvation Army lassie, resplendent in her bonnet, proudly announced: 'Sally Ann Chips – Potatoes the way they were meant to be.' After a while, import restrictions on food items were eased. The shops started to stock imported crisps. The customers dropped Sally Ann Chips in favour of Pringles and Walkers. But we were left with the name. 'Sally Ann' had become a household name with many in Dhaka. And 'Sally Ann' it would be when, soon after Mark's departure to Canada, the Army decided to go into serious business in Bangladesh.

Sally Ann café
– the place to
meet.

The pastry chef at the Dhaka Sheraton played an important part in the *Sally Ann* success story. Without his Black Forest cake there might never have been a story to tell.

It was December and only a few days more to go to Christmas. Not that many noticed in Dhaka. Christmas is not an event that draws much attention in Muslim Bangladesh. The Christians celebrate, of course, and the breaking news on state television on Christmas Day will be that 'this is the day that Jesus Christ was born'. The Prime Minister will receive Christian leaders in the garden of her official residence and cut the Christmas cake. That, too, will be duly reported on TV and in the papers. But apart from that, Christmas does not make much of a difference in the lives of people. No decorations, no great rush in the stores. No decorations, that is, except the illuminated advent star on the rooftops of a few houses announcing that here lives a Christian family, awaiting the birthday of Jesus. We went in search of some Christmas spirit and found it at the Dhaka Sheraton. Just inside the lobby door was Christ in the manger with Mary and Joseph, the kings and the shepherds, angels and donkeys and sheep all keeping their watch. Immediately behind them all was Santa Claus with his red-nosed reindeer. Next to him was a gleaming and glittering Christmas tree, complete with snow on the branches. Christmas, it seems, is cold and wintry, even in the tropics.

We had found what we had been looking for. It was Christmas and time to celebrate. We wanted a treat: the good, imported coffee they served at the Sheraton, and one of their cakes. The pastry chef had prepared a truly international array of Christmas goodies: Swedish ginger bread; German *Christstollen*; a *Gugelhopf* from Austria; moist and tempting Christmas pudding;

Wattapalam, the rich and sweet delicacy from Sri Lanka. It was not easy to choose. We looked at it all again. Finally, we ordered a piece of Black Forest cake. It was not especially 'christmassy', but it had something on top that we had not seen before in Bangladesh. Punctuated by a red, succulent cherry, there was a deliciously tempting, generous helping of whipped cream.

Bengalis like their food. Curries are prepared with great care. Spices are often mixed at home, with every housewife having her own secret mix. Fish, meat and vegetables – the ingredients must always be fresh. No meal is complete without a sweet. Everyone has their own favourite. Whether it is home made *chenna* – cheese balls – dripping in syrup, or a pudding of palm sugar, cashew nuts and raisins or simply some misty *dhoy* – sweet buffalo curd – they all have this in common: never is cream used in the preparation. Cream is not an ingredient, and it is certainly never used as 'whipped cream'. The explanation is probably to be found in the climate. It is hot, and refrigeration is a recent phenomenon. Cream could not be kept and was therefore never introduced into traditional Bengali cooking.

The Black Forest cake at the Sheraton was delicious. The cream tasted of 'home'. We asked the pastry chef where he bought the fresh cream. Maybe we could get it for special occasions. At the country's largest dairy farm, he told us. They used it in the production of butter, but kept some for the Sheraton, who were their only customer for fresh cream.

The date set for the opening of the *Sally Ann* shop at the Salvation Army Headquarters in Dhaka was 17 September 1997. It had become necessary to have our own outlet for the products that the women were making in Jessore and Old Dhaka. We had tried for some time to sell them to existing shops which marketed locally-produced handicrafts. There are a few in the capital. Some of them are quite large and also export to several countries. They had not been very willing to buy our goods. They would look at them, maybe buy a few, but that was usually the end of it. Often we would later find our designs copied and on display in their shops. We needed our own shop. One room was set aside and the date decided. The range of *Sally Ann* products was very limited. It was a long process to teach the women in the producer groups the need to change from traditional designs, and to ensure consistent quality and on-time delivery. A change of mind-set was needed. They were no longer recipients of development aid or charitable handouts. They were business partners.

It would be difficult to sustain a shop based on the available *Sally Ann* products. We needed something special to draw people, something that our target group wanted, but could not get anywhere else in Dhaka. Shopping in Dhaka involved travelling. There were no supermarkets that offered everything under one roof. One would buy yoghurt and rye bread at the Adventist shop, on display next to their beach mattresses and quilted bed covers. Fruit and vegetables were usually bought at the market, unless one wanted imported kiwis and strawberries. They were sold from a small stall outside the American Club and could be picked up on the way home from a game of tennis. The best corn on the cob was on offer there, too. For meat, one went to the German butcher (who was in fact from Hungary). He also sold ice cream and bread. 'King's Kitchen', a Chinese restaurant, was famous not for its lunches and dinners, but for the quality of its frozen fish, the variety of imported chilli sauces, baby clothes and its beauty salon. And, yes, its cinema that had a screening every Friday night. People travelled for their shopping. Getting people to the *Sally Ann* shop would not be difficult, if only we had something that would attract them.

Our thoughts went back to Christmas and the whipped cream at the Dhaka Sheraton. Surely, that could be the answer. Our market research had shown that our niche-market in Dhaka needed to be the expatriate community. We would not be able to compete with the established producers of traditional handicrafts. But no one made things that specifically appealed to people from the West and would fit into their home environment. We wanted to produce designs that they would want to buy and take home. We also looked ahead to possible export. Future *Sally*

Ann shops in the West would only succeed if they sold products that people wanted for their attractive designs. A customer would possibly buy something once to support a third world project; but she would not come back, unless it was to buy something that she really desired.

The few products we had ready for the opening of the *Sally Ann* Shop were designed for the expatriate community. Surely, fresh cream would also appeal to our target group! We missed it, we had enjoyed it at the Sheraton – we were not unique. Others would want it, too. The dairy was willing to sell it to us. We could buy as much as we wanted. They would make it available at their distribution outlet across town. We could collect it in a bucket in the morning and fill it in smaller containers back at the shop. The grand opening was advertised at all expatriate social clubs and embassies. 'Fresh Cream and Designer Products now available at The Salvation Army'. No one thought it strange. The mix was perfectly understandable to all.

The first customer was the Swedish ambassador's wife. She bought a jar of cream and looked at some handmade cards. She became one of our best supporters. As the range of products increased, she kept coming back. In the end, she and others would have more than 500 different products to choose from. Cards made from handmade paper; embroidered tablecloths, napkins and place mats; leaf-baskets and handbags; children's toys; wrought-iron chandeliers and lamp-stands; beautifully crafted furniture. The shop kept expanding and soon occupied the entire ground floor of the Headquarters building. We only took 700 takas the first week. That was less than 20 US dollars. But we were satisfied. People had come – and they kept coming back. They liked *Sally Ann* products. The designs and the quality of the products appealed to them. More women had to be employed in the production groups. The turnover increased steadily and *Sally Ann* started to be profitable.

People came for the products – and they never stopped coming for the fresh cream. It was the secret of success for the *Sally Ann* shop in Dhaka. Every morning it was collected on the back of a rickshaw from across town (in a cool-box to keep it fresh in the tropical heat) – and every day by early afternoon it was sold out. Embassies and expatriate clubs had standing orders. When Mövenpick Ice Cream opened their first outlet in Dhaka, they, too, became regular customers. At Christmas time people placed their orders long in advance. The *Sally Ann* Shop made it into the Dhaka guidebooks. It appeared in two listings: under the handicraft section for its wide selection of designer goods and under the food section for the place to buy fresh cream.

Sally Ann opened its own café after a while. The menu was limited. Tea or coffee, and Norwegian waffles with whipped cream. Furniture and décor was all produced in-house. Soon it became the place to meet for a good cup of coffee with friends or to read *Homes and Gardens* and *The War Cry*. We often send a grateful thought to the pastry chef at the Sheraton. Without his Black Forest cake, there might never have been a *Sally Ann* story to tell.

Quality control,
Sally Ann knitting
factory, Savar.

5 CHANGED LIVES – YARN FROM NORWAY

There were plenty of smiles and tears during the first graduation ceremony at the training centre of The Salvation Army's knitting factory in Savar. The initial group of trainees, 20 women in all, had completed their course and were ready to leave for employment in one of the many commercial textile factories in the area. Textiles have overtaken jute as Bangladesh's main foreign export earner. There is a demand for skilled labourers. True, the market will always be volatile. Foreign buyers go where the cost is lowest. A slump in the economies of the West has an immediate effect in the factories of Asia. But for years to come, it would be safe to foresee a reasonable growth in employment opportunities in the textile industry. The women who proudly received their certificates that day, should be able to earn a living.

The day was a remarkable achievement, both for the trainees and for The Salvation Army in Bangladesh. For the trainees, it marked the end of a journey that had started in the brothels and on the streets of Old Dhaka. For the Army, the journey included places like San Pedro in California, Stavanger and Bergen in Norway, Hong Kong and mainland China. The day could not have happened without the internationalism of The Salvation Army.

There were smiles of pride and joy. The group before us looked like any group of young women in Bangladesh. They were dressed for the occasion in their most colourful saris. Their hair was neatly arranged and glass-beaded bangles and earrings complemented the picture. They looked very different when we first met. They had all worked as sex workers then, in the horrid brothels or on the narrow and crowded streets of Old Dhaka.

The Army moved into Old Dhaka in 1995. The agenda was HIV/AIDS. The target was the largest of the Dhaka brothels. More than a thousand women worked under conditions that were inhumane and degrading and clearly a threat to their health and that of their customers – to say nothing of the many children who lived in the brothel. We saw children drugged, so they would sleep under their mother's bed while she was entertaining her customers. We wanted to find a way into the brothel for the children's sake, too. The Salvation Army's troops for the initial attack consisted of five or six people. The tactics were simple. We walked into the community and talked to people. Our first meeting was in a small workshop, directly opposite the entrance to the brothel. They produced metal furniture. Work went on as we had our conversation with the owner and several interested people who walked in off the street. The noise was unbearable at times, with metal sheets being cut and bent and steel frames being welded together. The noise did not stop people from talking. They shared our concern for the brothel and what it did to the ladies who worked there and to their community. They could help us get into the brothel. They knew the owner. Off we marched across the street, the Salvation Army group and our new-found community partners.

It was not easy to make an impact in the brothel in Old Dhaka. The Army hired a small room in the brothel itself and a team of workers visited every day. It was a question of forming relationships and building trust. People are used to being exploited in the brothel. Survival depends on self-preservation. Trusting relationships are not the norm. But slowly the Army workers were tolerated, if not accepted. Some of the sex workers started to confide in the women in the blue saris. We could help some of the children. After a while it no longer became practical to keep the room in the brothel. A nearby office was found. The staff continued to visit as before.

There was unrest in the brothel. The talk was of closing down. Rumour had it that the owner wanted his buildings back so he could use them for a different purpose. The girls protested. They claimed they had rights. They fulfilled a role in society. They had been tolerated by all until now. No one had the right to expel them. It became a political issue. The papers wrote about the brothels in Dhaka. Politicians denied they existed. NGOs had their say. All the while, the ladies feared for their livelihood and the future of their children.

One early morning a mob attacked the brothel. It was said the owner of the property had hired them. The girls had to flee, leaving their belongings behind. Some were barefoot, some were in their nightclothes. It was the dramatic end of the largest brothel in Old Dhaka.

Our project staff walked around the area, keeping a careful distance from the brothel where the mob were still engaged in looting whatever had been left behind. Would this be the end of our involvement in Old Dhaka? Our staff spotted one or two of the girls they knew from the brothel, hiding as best they could in the back streets. 'What can we do now?' they asked. 'We need a fresh start.' That same day it was decided to reshape the Army's programme in Old Dhaka. We would offer the girls a fresh start. No one knew what or how, but it seemed right and so it was done.

For the ladies who graduated in Savar, the traumatic events of that day were still a painful memory. But it had faded into the background. They had experienced that good came from bad. They had found the Army's new office the following day. They already knew the staff. Together, they started to rearrange their lives and look for new options.

The office in Old Dhaka became an advice centre and a social club. Anything between 60 and 80 of the former brothel ladies would visit during the day. The room was soon too small and a larger one was found. Children started to come with their mothers. The staff helped them find a school in the vicinity. Many of the girls continued in street prostitution. We needed to find ways to help them into alternative employment.

The Regent Hall Salvation Army Corps in London has a prestigious location in Oxford Street. Paul Pirie was employed to run the corps bookstore. Paul was keenly interested in Fairtrade issues. He had written a paper on the topic for the Army's international leaders. But he also approached the subject from a practical angle. He wanted to sell cards and other goods that had been produced by Salvation Army projects in poor countries. We had met Paul and shown him some cards that were now on sale in the one-room *Sally Ann* shop in Dhaka. Paul liked the quality. He wanted us to produce Christmas cards with designs that he would provide, and he placed a substantial order. Two ladies had started to make them in the production room in the garage behind Headquarters. Now it was decided to involve the Old Dhaka ladies in this production. They were taught the art of card-cutting, and so it transpired that cards from the Salvation Army centre in English Road in Old Dhaka were sold in Oxford Street, London. The orders from Regent Hall soon stopped, however. Paul Pirie would have liked to continue. There was disagreement over how the law in England should be interpreted. Did Regent Hall Corps have the right to import Salvation Army goods, or was that right reserved for The Salvation Army Trading Company in the UK? The issue was never resolved and this promising enterprise came to a close. We were sorry to lose our best overseas customer at the time.

Halfway across the world, a meeting took place that would be hugely significant for the ladies in Old Dhaka. The Salvation Army held its International Recycling Conference in San Pedro, California. The Hilton on the San Pedro waterfront is far removed from the squalor of Old Dhaka. Yet the people who gathered there were equally mission-minded as were the Army's workers in Dhaka. The Salvation Army has a large share of the world's market in second-hand clothing. It does not just happen for the sake of business. It serves the purposes of the Army's mission.

We were there to explore a possible way for the Army to enter the lucrative market for second-hand clothing in Bangladesh. It did not look good. People who exported clothing for the Army all over the world did not want to touch Bangladesh. 'Too corrupt,' they said. 'The market is tightly controlled by a few who will stop at nothing to protect their monopoly.' It seemed we would leave San Pedro with a negative result.

Kjell Inge Olsen is a life-long Salvationist and a successful businessman from Norway. Ever the optimist, he has been an entrepreneur all his working life, always ready to try what no one has tried before. Mr Olsen attended the San Pedro conference as the Managing Director of Fretex Vest, a part of the Army's Fretex group of companies in Norway. Fretex is a market leader in recycling in Norway, helping hundreds of people who need a fresh start in the job market in the process. He was presenting Fretex's latest project to the conference delegates. They had invented a process by which the very last leftovers of the recycling process – that which could not be sold even as rags – were processed into yarn. The yarn was used to knit socks and sweaters at a knitting factory in Norway.

Could the knitting be done in Bangladesh? Could the Army in Norway provide the yarn to a Salvation Army knitting factory in Bangladesh? Could the end product be sent back to Norway for sale in Fretex shops? We were talking over lunch on the final day of the conference. It seemed an unlikely scheme. It had never been done before. Huge distances were involved. The Army in Bangladesh did not have a knitting factory. Who did we have capable of getting a knitting factory off the ground? Where would the investment capital come from? There were plenty of reasons not to pursue the idea any further. Indeed, it would have seemed sensible not to pursue the idea any further. Mr Olsen was of a different mind. He did not look for the things that could go wrong. That is easy. Anyone can think of a hundred reasons why new and untested ideas should not work. In fact, that seems to be a common approach in many a Salvation Army boardroom, as in the boardrooms of large insitutions the world over. How much could be achieved if there were more daring!

Mr Olsen did not let the idea rest. Soon, a plan took shape. A letter of intent was signed. Fretex would supply the recycled yarn and pay for the return freight to Norway. The Salvation Army in Bangladesh would start a knitting factory and provide employment for former sex workers from Old Dhaka. It was a wild idea, really, but it felt right and it was exciting. We registered the project with the Board of Investment of the Government of Bangladesh. That was the first step. The rest, we believed, would fall into place.

Mr Stig Sperrevik, a Norwegian Salvationist, had worked for the Army in Bangladesh as a volunteer for a year and a half. His initial intention was to come for six months to install a computer network at Headquarters. He liked what he was doing and stayed on, training people in computer use and software design. Now he had made up his mind to return to his career as a computer programmer in Norway. He changed his decision when he was asked to start a knitting factory. He signed up for two more years. Once you are in Bangladesh, it is not easy to leave! Bangladesh offers excitement and opportunities that cannot be found anywhere else. Where else would a computer programmer be asked to plan and start a knitting factory?

We now had a Board of Investment registration, a project manager and the promise of yarn from Norway. It was a good start, but still a long way to go. Here is the remaining story in short: The Salvation Army in the USA pledged the investment capital; Mr Knut Johan Onarheim, a lawyer who served on the Board of Directors of Fretex and who had been involved in setting up a knitting factory for the handicapped in China, visited twice to offer expert advice; a wing of the Savar Children's Home was converted into a factory; machinery was imported from Hong Kong; all licenses were obtained without payment of bribes (we needed at least 10 official licenses, nobody thought it could be done without paying 'service fees' – the process was difficult and was the cause of many frustrations!); staff were recruited; the yarn arrived and was cleared through customs (that was a difficult and frustrating process, too). The Salvation Army Knitting Factory in Savar was a miracle, proof that the improbable should be attempted and that the seemingly impossible can happen.

The ladies from Old Dhaka arrived for their first working day. Savar was a world away from their usual environment of Old Dhaka. They felt uncomfortable. They looked out of place. They still wore make-up and dressed the way they had in the brothel. It was plain for all to see that they were different from their new neighbours. Few could read or write, or even count. It is necessary to be able to count in English to be able to operate a commercial knitting machine. The patterns are recorded that way. The training would have to be very basic and very thorough. It would take a lot of effort.

The ladies who smiled their smiles and cried their tears at their graduation ceremony were changed people. There was no more exaggerated make-up. They looked like any group of young women in Bangladesh. Their very appearance had changed. But the change was not only external. There was a look of self-esteem and dignity as they stepped up to receive their diplomas. Girls who had not been able to read and write now proudly read to each other the simple text of their training certificates. The girls smiled. They were proud; they had achieved so much. They cried. There were tears of sorrow; they would have to leave their friends. But mostly they cried tears of joy. The old life was behind them. They'd had a new start. The future was bright. The Salvation Army staff smiled and cried with them.

The yarn from Norway had been made into sweaters. However, this batch was never sent back to Fretex. A particularly cold winter caused much suffering in northern Bangladesh. 'Send them there,' was the generous message from Norway. Five thousand warm, woollen sweaters. They had already made such a difference in the lives of the people who had produced them. Now they were passed on to others who depended on them for their very survival.

Fretex involvement has come to an end. The Salvation Army factory now produces for *Sally Ann*. Stig has long since handed over to John Litu Das, a local Salvationist whom he trained as a manager. Young women are still being trained for future employment in the commercial sector. As part of their training, they produce cushion covers, blankets and children's clothing that can be bought in the *Sally Ann* shops in Dhaka and Oslo.

One serious impediment to the commercial success of the Knitting Factory had remained throughout. When the authorities gave their approval for The Salvation Army to open the factory, they imposed the condition that only recycled yarn from Norway was to be used in the production, and that all finished products would have to be exported to Norway. The training aspect could take place, of course, but it was difficult to make the factory financially viable under those conditions. Lieut-Colonel Ethne Flintoff, a New Zealand Salvation Army officer who has spent over 25 years in India, Pakistan and Bangladesh, inherited this problem when she took over the leadership of The Salvation Army in Bangladesh in 2002. For two years, she has tried to get a waiver on all conditions. The application has done the rounds of the Board of Investment (BOI), the Bangladesh Garments' Manufacturers and Exporters Association and the NGO Affairs Bureau. It was not looking at all hopeful. In fact, it looked *hopeless*.

The final crucial meeting of the directors of the BOI took place, one Saturday in August 2004. Ethne heard of the meeting on the Thursday evening. A volunteer had told her about it – a Muslim gentleman who is in sympathy with the Army's work and who had been helping her for some time to pursue the matter. He had worked hard, visiting offices and knocking on doors – being importunate. Now there was nothing more he could do to help. They decided that they could do nothing but pray. Ethne's faith was weak. It seemed like a lost cause. But she prayed despite her feelings. She knew she prayed to the God of all possibilities. The decision of the meeting was an unconditional waiver of all conditions.

Ethne was strengthened in her assurance that God is in control of the affairs of The Salvation Army in Bangladesh. He had stamped his seal of approval on the Army's knitting factory in Savar when he married the needs of commercial sex workers in Old Dhaka with an unlikely idea in the minds of two conference delegates in California. He will see it through.

Knitting factory – trainees at the linking machines.

Children at the
Salvation Army,
Savar Integrated
Children's Centre.

The Army's world leaders had announced a visit to Bangladesh. General Paul Rader and Commissioner Kay Rader would spend four days in the country. Kay Rader, especially, had shown a keen interest in the *Sally Ann* project. She was intrigued by the thought that sex workers from Old Dhaka were taught new skills and given a chance of a better life. The *Sally Ann* Shop at Headquarters had only been open a few months. She wanted to see it so that she could possibly promote *Sally Ann* products on her travels around the world. She also wanted to meet some of the girls from Old Dhaka. The shop was still only one room. True, it had developed quite well in the short time since its opening. Sales were considerably up from the 700-taka turnover during the first week. There was a steady flow of customers and new products were being added to the stock all the time. Yet it was still all in one room. Not much to show to one who had a global view! It was decided to expand. We would add a room and make sure that all new design ideas were produced and on display by the time the Raders were due.

Bangladesh is an interesting mix of great efficiency and hopeless ineffectiveness. Things go wrong all the time, but there is always a way to put them right. The Raders' visit would give us ample opportunity to experience this. Things can happen very fast in Bangladesh. People are industrious and willing to work hard. It is usually the red tape that stops things.

The Salvation Army in Bangladesh was still a young organisation. It had not yet created much red tape. The distance from decision-making to implementation was very short. Therefore, expansion was possible. *Orders & Regulations* (the detailed rules by which The Salvation Army manages things) and various organisational departments were not in the way. People walked out of the boardroom as soon as a decision had been made and began to implement it straight away. It was decided to expand – and that is what happened. The visit by the General and Commissioner Rader marked an expansion of the Army's work in Bangladesh in more ways than one.

It was the afternoon before their arrival. The 60 Salvationists of Dhaka – all of them – were together for a final rehearsal of the welcome ceremony. The programme brief for the four days had been planned and rehearsed. We were confident that every eventuality had been thought of. We had it all in hand; the international visitors would be well taken care of from the moment of their arrival until they would leave for India. The phone rang; it was the General Manager of the Pan Pacific Sonargaon hotel. He phoned to inform us that they no longer had any rooms for the General and his party. The Prime Minister had decided to invite her Indian and Pakistani counterparts for a summit meeting. They would arrive the following morning, and the government had commandeered every available hotel room in Dhaka. It would be no use phoning the Sheraton, he said. They, too, had asked all their guests to vacate by the evening.

The Prime Ministerial summit was a political sensation. Rarely did the heads of government of India and Pakistan meet. It was a hopeful sign for South Asian relations. For our own top-level visit it was complicating in the extreme. The visitors were due in less than 12 hours and we had no accommodation for them.

The General had been granted VIP status by the government. That would ease entry formalities at the airport and secure an official security escort throughout their stay. We reached the Chief Protocol Officer of the government on the phone. He understood our predicament. Also, it would not reflect well on the Government of Bangladesh if one of their official VIP guests was left stranded. He promised we could have two rooms at the Sonargaon. He would inform the hotel himself and ensure that the security people knew that they should let us in.

The General and Commissioner Rader arrived. The journey from the airport took much longer than usual. As we approached the hotel, there were unprecedented levels of security. Roadblocks manned by elite marines; armoured vehicles and anti aircraft guns at strategic positions around the building; secret service agents everywhere, easily recognisable by their dark sunglasses and earpieces. The prime ministers of India and Pakistan have enemies. No one was to be allowed to threaten them during their summit in Bangladesh. The hotel's General Manager was ready with a red carpet welcome and flowers for the General and Commissioner Rader. Somehow, all the 60 Salvationists had been allowed in. A ballroom was allocated for the welcome ceremony and the visitors were welcomed again with ceremonial dances and more flowers. It was time to go to the rooms, which we were informed were on the seventh floor, the Executive Floor. There was only one other guest on that floor, the Pakistani Prime Minister, Mr Sharif.

When we stepped out of the lift, we were met by two Pakistani security guards with machine guns. Commissioner Rader's handbag and flowers were taken away for inspection. The Pakistani chief security officer was called. It soon became evident that they were far from welcoming. They would allow no one onto the floor where their Prime Minister was staying. It did not matter that the guests were VIP visitors of the Bangladeshi government. This was understandable; they were only doing their duty. They were responsible for their own Prime Minister's security and no one was getting near him.

We beat a retreat in the lift down to the hotel lobby. Frantic discussions with the General Manager resulted in two rooms being found. Just how he did it, with every room being taken, we do not know. It was another example of the great efficiency with which problems are overcome in Bangladesh. We were happy; we had made it to the hotel and we had two rooms.

Would the Prime Minister still see us? Sheikh Hasina had agreed to a half-hour meeting at her official residence. The arrangements had been made long before the Prime Ministers' summit

had been announced, of course. We were prepared for a call to say that it could no longer take place. No call came. The Christian businessman, who had helped us with the arrangements, must be more influential than we had realised!

We arrived at the prime ministerial residence and were ushered into the reception room. At the agreed time, the Honourable Prime Minister Sheikh Hasina entered. Politicians in Asia often represent a political dynasty. That is certainly true for women politicians and explains why countries like Pakistan, Bangladesh, India, Sri Lanka and Indonesia all have or have had women leaders. Benazir Bhutto of Pakistan, Sheikh Hasina and Begum Khaleda Zia of Bangladesh, Indira Gandhi and Sonia Gandhi of India, Mrs. Sirimavo Bandaranaike – the 'weeping widow' who became the world's first female prime minister – and her daughter Chandrika Kumaratunga of Sri Lanka and Megawatti Sukarnoputri of Indonesia all held their posts as representatives of a political family. This does not necessarily mean that they are not capable politicians themselves. It does mean that they come to the post with added power and influence.

Sheikh Hasina is the daughter of Sheikh Mujibur Rahman – Bangabandhu, the father of the modern nation of Bangladesh. He was assassinated together with most of his family in August 1975. Hasina and a sister survived. They were studying in Germany at the time. Sheikh Hasina's political agenda has been strongly influenced by the tragic events of 1975. She has sought to bring the alleged killers to justice. The reception room was filled with photographs of her late father and other members of her family.

We stood as she entered. She had obviously not had time to read the briefing papers. We heard her ask her aide who her uniformed visitors were as she approached us. That was understandable, given the busy schedule of the political summit. We were just grateful that she went ahead with the meeting. We could inform the Prime Minister that her father had been most generous in his support of The Salvation Army. Major Eva den Hartog, the legendary Dutch Salvation

Army officer who was in charge of the Army's work during Bangladesh's first years as a nation, met with him on a regular basis. The Salvation Army had also organised an irrigation scheme for farmers in Sheikh Hasina's home village, a scheme that was still ongoing after nearly 25 years.

It was a good meeting for the Army. It represented an expansion of our profile in the public eye when the meeting was reported in the evening news, immediately following a report on the political summit. The General and Commissioner Rader appeared alongside the Prime Minister and the Army's work was described.

The most significant moment happened away from the cameras, though. The General had exchanged gifts with the Prime Minister. We were preparing to leave. Sheikh Hasina assured us of her government's full support for our work. General Rader expressed our sincere prayers for the Almighty's blessings upon the Prime Minister and her government, on her family and on the nation of Bangladesh.

She looked genuinely moved then, Prime Minister Sheikh Hasina. Politicians in South Asia are used to operating in a hostile environment. Maybe she needed that meeting as part of her political summit. Maybe she needed someone to pray for her and wish her well. Maybe she needed someone to remind her of the Almighty to whom we all shall answer. Maybe The Salvation Army has a special mission in Bangladesh to 'pray for those in authority'.

Next on the agenda was a visit to Jessore, the stronghold of Salvation Army work in Bangladesh. Jessore is a half-hour flight West of Dhaka. By road the journey can take anything between eight and 15 hours, depending on the totally unpredictable ferry across the mighty Padma river. The General and his party would fly. Biman Bangladesh Airlines held the monopoly on all flight concessions in the country. They had a fleet of 10 aircraft to service all international and domestic routes. Presently, all but two were grounded. One had crashed into a rice field on approach to

Sylhet airport (fortunately and miraculously without serious injury to passengers and crew); the others all had technical problems. The two aircraft that were deemed airworthy were busily dashing around the skies to try and keep up the schedules. Needless to say, there were serious delays on all routes. Missionary Aviation Fellowship (MAF) came to our rescue. They had been given permission to fly ambulance flights and private charter for NGOs and we booked their eight-seater deHavilland for the short flight to Jessore.

The General's visit took place in January. The nights were cool and in the morning there was the danger of thick fog that could often linger for hours. Fortunately, this morning looked fairly clear. There should be no delays in getting to Jessore. We checked into the VIP lounge at the domestic airport and waited for MAF's Swedish pilot to come. When he did, it was with bad news. Air traffic control would not allow us to fly due to low visibility on approach to Jessore. The pilot argued that both he and the aircraft were equipped for these conditions. It did not help. We were grounded. The hours passed slowly. It was in the middle of the holy month of Ramadan. Out of courtesy to our Muslim hosts who were fasting, we could not serve any food or drink to our guests. Three hours passed before we could finally take to the skies. Ironically, a minute before us, Biman's old ATP took off for Jessore.

One thousand five hundred children from the Army's primary schools were lining the streets as the General's motorcade drove into Jessore. They had been waiting since the early morning. The long wait had not dampened their enthusiasm. They waved flags and showered the visitors with flowers. A guard of honour of armed policemen greeted the VIP guests when they arrived at the Salvation Army compound. The programme had to be curtailed. A planned visit to the Army's brothel programme was cancelled. By now, the girls in the brothel would be just too busy with their customers to receive any visitors. There was still time for a visit to the village of Ghurulia before the public meeting later in the afternoon. In a short time, the Corps in Ghurulia had enrolled over 100 soldiers. The Army had started a school and a clinic. The villagers are poor people, mostly day labourers. They depended on their daily income. They could not afford to take a day off every week to come for worship at the corps. The Corps Officers solved the problem. They would pray with their soldiers every morning before they went to the fields. They would meet them again in the evening when they returned. There was daily worship at the corps in Ghurulia. Today, everybody had taken a day off. They were all out to greet the General. They were proud to be Salvationists.

The day in Jessore ended with a public meeting. A tent-like *shamiyana* had been erected in the grounds of the local Roman Catholic Church. Three thousand people came. It was the largest Christian meeting ever to be held in that part of Bangladesh. Expansion.

The final day would be very busy. Early morning, the visitors were received at the *Sally Ann* shop. The expansion had been completed in time. The second room was filled with new products. The General and Commissioner Rader took their time. They looked and photographed and asked questions. Kay Rader placed the largest order for *Sally Ann* products to date. She wanted her official Christmas gifts for all international women leaders of The Salvation Army that year to be supplied by *Sally Ann.*

Later, the Raders walked through the slums of Mirpur. Micro-credit was the focus of the visit. This had only just been added to the Army's working agenda in Mirpur. It has since grown into a large-scale project that has helped hundreds of people establish a source of income. We called at the first loan-taker's little workplace. It was in a corner of the small room he occupied with his wife and their five children. He had invented a procedure for re-filling disposable ballpoint pens. They sold well in the local market. He was able to send his children to school and still repay the loan he had taken.

'How much money do you have available for this scheme?' the General wanted to know. We told him. 'Could you do with an additional 5,000 dollars?' he asked. We certainly could, and thanked him as we walked on through the narrow lanes. Open sewers ran on either side. Heaps of rubbish lay uncollected, attracting flies in their thousands and spreading disease. Goats, dogs and chickens competed with the children for the scarce space between the houses. The General must have seen it all before. Slums are not unique to Dhaka. They exist as concentrations of poverty in every mega-city around the world. Here, in the slums of Mirpur, The Salvation Army actively sought to address the problems of poverty. It impressed the General. By the end of the Mirpur tour he had pledged not 5,000 but 30,000 dollars from Salvation Army international resources to expand the micro-credit facilities to as many as possible. The General's dollars have since revolved many times. The value of the initial sum has multiplied as loans have been taken and repaid. The General's visit that day continues to result in improved lives for some of Dhaka's poor.

The visit would be concluded with a public meeting in Dhaka. It had been decided to hire the large Methodist church. It was the largest church building around, capable of holding 1,800 people. It was the first time that The Salvation Army would invite the public to such a large meeting in Dhaka. The 60 Salvationists in the capital were confident that the hall could be filled.

People started to arrive hours before the meeting. It soon became clear that the faith of the Salvationists would be honoured. There was not an empty seat to be found. In the congregation was a group of ladies from Old Dhaka. Sex workers from the Army's project; *Sally Ann* workers; Kay Rader's crowd, the ladies she wanted to meet. They had never before been to a Christian meeting. They had come with the project workers, out of respect for the woman who was so interested in them and the things they produced.

One minute before the meeting was due to start, the electricity went off. Power cuts are a common feature of life in Bangladesh. Power generation cannot keep up with a growing demand. The distribution systems are old and frequently fail. The emergency generator would take care of it. We would only need to wait for a minute or two, and the generator would come on. It did not happen. The darkness was complete. The ceiling fans had stopped working and it was becoming uncomfortably warm. The emergency generator had failed.

We marched in front of the Army's international leaders into the first major public Salvation Army meeting in Dhaka. The hall was filled to capacity. We could not see anyone. All we had to illuminate the hall was one candle. We held it aloft and shielded its flame – and somehow it was sufficient. Silence spread throughout the hall as the little light proceeded to the front and the meeting commenced.

More candles were found, a few torches hurriedly bought at the nearest market. Life goes on in Bangladesh whatever happens. People find ways around temporary setbacks. The power returned as the General got up to speak. The gospel message worked powerfully on the crowd. The first people to accept the invitation to the Mercy Seat, the Army's place of prayer, were the ladies from Old Dhaka. They knelt with their project workers. They found the Lord. *Sally Ann* is more than a business. It is mission. It is Kingdom-expansion.

Sally Ann production group in Konejpur village. Visitors: Jan Størksen, Reidar Lorentzen, May-Britt Lyngroth, flanked by Bo and Birgitte Brekke.

It soon became clear that *Sally Ann* needed an overseas market. Our in-country operations were profitable, but there was limited growth potential. The market in Dhaka was by no means exhausted, yet *Sally Ann* could grow only to a point by keeping to the domestic market. If we wanted to grow big, we would need to find an overseas partner.

There is nothing like trying! We tried all our contacts. *Sally Ann* products were soon on sale in one way or other in places as far apart as Stockholm and Singapore, and London and Los Angeles. There were interested enquiries from other places, too. The Army in Hong Kong wondered if they could be helpful. We communicated with officers in Australia and Switzerland. It was very much a question of trial and failure. Much trial and much failure. Somehow, every attempt ran into difficulties and died an unprofitable death. We needed something better.

Major Inger Marit Nygård has been visiting Bangladesh regularly for many years. She serves as the Project Officer for The Salvation Army in Norway. When she was appointed to the job, she had hardly been across the border to Sweden. She had no experience of working in Third World countries, nor did she have any relevant education to qualify her for the job. Yet some Army leader must have been in tune with God. And God said: Inger Marit is my woman for this task. It is doubtful that Inger Marit would have identified 'development work' as her spiritual gifting or thought of herself as especially suited to co-ordinate complex negotiations between government agencies and Salvation Army territories around the world. How wrong we are, sometimes, to define our spiritual gifts! How we limit God when we tell him what we are good at! God is looking for obedience. He wants people who are willing to try. If it looks impossible, all the better! Attempt it, if that is what God the Almighty asks of you! Major Nygård was willing to try and she is doing outstanding work. She has developed an eye for the real needs of a situation. She has been able to channel millions of dollars to worthy projects around the world.

Inger Marit came to evaluate the Army's HIV/AIDS Project in Bangladesh. NORAD, the Norwegian Government's development agency was paying 80 per cent of the project costs. The Army's Norway Territory picked up the balance. A programme of teaching and prevention through community counselling impacts on all Salvation Army activities in Bangladesh. Every corps and every health and development project is impacted. Even at Headquarters, there are discussions on issues relating to risk behaviours and prevention. Major Nygård had been visiting Old Dhaka. She had seen how former prostitutes were making cards for *Sally Ann*. She saw the impact on their lives. She also understood the limitations of the local market.

'What you need,' she said, 'is to get Jan Størksen and Thor Fjellvang to visit. Leave it with me; I will arrange it.' We did not know it at the time, but Inger Marit had just opened the door to an exciting new development for *Sally Ann*. She had opened the door to the world. That which we had been trying so hard to achieve was about to be provided: an overseas partner who would set *Sally Ann* on the road to achieving its global vision.

Both Jan and Thor are Salvationists who work for the Army in Norway. Jan was the head of the marketing department at Territorial Headquarters. Thor was managing the Army's recycling business, Fretex, in the south-east of the country. In recent years, The Salvation Army in Norway has successfully re-defined its public image. The 'Army brand' has become fashionable without having sacrificed any of its values. Soup, soap and salvation – the old Army catchphrase – are current words. Fretex has become a market leader in recycling, changing lives and influencing government policy in the process. Jan and Thor have been key people in these processes. 'You need them to visit Bangladesh,' Inger Marit Nygård said. She was right.

They soon arrived in Dhaka; Jan, with his marketing genius; Thor with his business-realism. They brought the right mix of qualities. They were God's answer to our needs. The Salvation Army is richly blessed with human resources. They are not all in one place, but globally we have them. We must get better at bringing them to the point of need in our global mission.

Jan and Thor fell in love with Bangladesh. They were spared none of the realities of poor people's lives. We took them to the brothels and the slums. They spent time in the villages and in the busiest parts of the cities. They saw for themselves the purpose of *Sally Ann*: to provide a way out for some of the world's poor. They came to understand the essence of fair trade. They saw the face of poverty – and *Sally Ann* became a mission, a labour of love for them.

Thor and Jan set to work. Armed with their vision and energised by their new-found love, they shared their enthusiasm with others. People became involved. Soon, a host of professional people had joined the *Sally Ann* team in Norway. The vision appealed to them: Fairtrade as a practical response to the problem of poverty; The Salvation Army uniquely positioned through its existing international network to become a global leader in the fight against poverty. Here was a cause that was both grand and achievable. People wanted to be involved.

Mr Reidar Lorentzen is the Director of the Kavli Trust. He administers large sums of money that the Kavli Company, one of Norway's major food processing companies, each year sets aside for humanitarian work. In fact, all the profits from the company go to charitable work or are re-invested in the company. There are no shareholders, no one who gets rich. The Kavli Trust has been a major supporter of The Salvation Army's work for years. Reidar understood the concepts and the potential of *Sally Ann*. He offered his business expertise and financial support from the Kavli Trust. Later, when '*Sally Ann* Norway Ltd' was incorporated, he became one of its directors.

Mr Erling Johannes Ølstad, an entrepreneur who has built up a countrywide chain of flower shops, joined him. He now has close on 60 stores. He knew what was needed to launch a brand. He also had practical experience of fair-trade operations in the developing world. The roses for his shops are all supplied from Tanzania.

Nina Jernberg works for the marketing company Uniform – an apt name for someone who wants to work for The Salvation Army, she would say. Nina was asked to develop a logo and a visual concept that would capture the spirit and purpose of *Sally Ann*. She put more than her professional know-how into the task. Her heart was in this. She had been asked to give expression to a vision. She soon found herself immersed in the enthusiasm of the team. All throughout the market research and design process, when thinking about target groups and logo and colours, Nina would feel part of a cause.

Mr Knut Bry is a photographer of world fame. His works have been exhibited in the best galleries. He has worked for the most famous of fashion magazines. He constantly travels the world, maintaining only a small room in Oslo as his base. Knut has a heart for the world's poor. He meets them on all his travels. He volunteered to shoot the photos for a book Jan planned, which would highlight the work of *Sally Ann* in Bangladesh. *Soap* it was called; the second in a trilogy, *Soup, Soap, Salvation*. A well known journalist and author, Mr Vetle Lid Larssen wrote the text.

Linda Sande is Knut Bry's stylist. She has worked with him on many projects. She would work with him on *Soap*. Later, she continued her involvement with *Sally Ann*. She worked with Jan Størksen on a fashion show that would feature recycled clothing from Fretex combined with textiles from Bangladesh. Top models walked the catwalk in the Army's Temple Corps in Oslo – an event that caused great media attention and raised many eyebrows.

Peter Løchstøer is one of Norway's best known textile designers. In 2003 he won first prize at the Oslo Fashion Week. The values Peter saw in the *Sally Ann* concept reflected his own. He has made himself available and is now in charge of product development for *Sally Ann*. Through Peter Løchstøer, other designers from Norway are becoming involved in product design.

Many more could be mentioned. The entire Salvation Army in Norway seemed to be involved; the territorial leaders, Jan's marketing-colleagues, Thor's board members in Fretex. They all worked on the *Sally Ann* plans in addition to their busy workloads. The energy and vision were catching on.

There were numerous visits to Bangladesh. Jan and Thor came back. Nina came and Reidar came. Knut Bry spent a week in the country as did Mr Larssen, the journalist. With Jan, Peter Løchstøer has travelled extensively both in Bangladesh and Africa, sometimes spending weeks at a time meeting with producers, searching the local markets for available materials, looking for inspiration in the meeting of cultures. There were further meetings in Oslo. Logo and design had been agreed, all aimed to appeal to the chosen target group. A business concept was developed that would allow for future franchising.

Commissioners Donald and Berit Ødegaard, Army leaders with many years' service in Africa and now in charge of the Army's work in Norway, agreed to the incorporation of a Salvation Army-owned '*Sally Ann* Norway Ltd'. Berit joined the board of directors. A shop in a Salvation Army building in a prominent location was made available. The first shipment of *Sally Ann* products was ordered from Bangladesh. Wooden toys from Tanzania and coffee from the Army's farm in Kenya were added. In August 2002 the first *Sally Ann* Shop in Oslo was opened by Ms Hilde Frafjord Johnsen, the Norwegian Government Minister in charge of international development.

We could only marvel at the level of involvement people displayed. *Sally Ann* had come a long way from its small beginnings as a failed sewing project in Jessore. The products now on sale in Oslo were featured in the best interior design magazines in the country. It proves what can happen when people armed with a vision and energised by love set to work.

Nothing can replace the coming-together of people. It ought to be our leadership mantra: bring people together. There is no better way to ensure progress in mission. Get people to meet on any issue, and creative energy will take over. The creator God has made it that way. Thor and Jan and the *Sally Ann* team from Bangladesh dreamed and made plans. When they left, a broad and colourful picture had been painted. It was inspired optimism. Realism would soon enough have its say. It was good to start with a vision.

Vision is important. When the views of reality want to dim the picture, a clear vision is needed that will shine bright and be the guiding-light, the goal to aim for, the dream to fulfil.

The vision for *Sally Ann* has since been clearly stated: *Through Sally Ann, The Salvation Army will become a global driving force for developing profitable, fair trade.* It was not as clear as that when the Norwegian visitors left for home. But in essence the vision was there: what had started in Bangladesh would spread across the world and develop into a global network involving as many Salvation Army countries as possible in mission-focussed trading. The Bangladesh-Norway link would prove to the world that it was possible.

Sally Ann shop in Oslo, Norway – and some products.

8 THE 'SALVATION ARMY' BROTHEL!

The Salvation Army has been working with commercial sex workers from its very early days. This is not surprising. Prostitution is, after all, the world's oldest trade. It existed in Victorian England as it exists in today's world, in every country where the movement is at work. Whatever form the Army's work has taken – rescue homes, midnight patrols, counselling services, advocacy and lobbying – there has always been much compassion and little condemnation. For sure, The Salvation Army has occasionally spoken strongly against injustices that lead to the exploitation of vulnerable people and laws that fail to protect them, but there has always been much compassion for the prostitute. That is how it should be. The prostitute is a victim, often of circumstance and always of other people.

William Booth's language may no longer be politically correct when he talks of 'fallen women', but there can be no misunderstanding his compassion when he writes in 1885: 'And when once the poor girl has consented to buy the right to earn her living by the sacrifice of her virtue, then she is treated as a slave and an outcast by the very men who have ruined her. Her word becomes unbelievable, her life an ignominy, and she is swept downward ever downward, into the bottomless perdition of prostitution. But there, even in the lowest depths, excommunicated by Humanity and outcast from God, she is far nearer the pitying heart of the One true Saviour than all the men who forced her down, aye, and than all the Pharisees and Scribes who stand silently by while these fiendish wrongs are perpetrated before their very eyes.' He urged his troops on to an 'immediate formation' of a response that would centre on London, but 'as soon as possible' spread to Paris, New York, Chicago, Toronto, Melbourne, Sydney, 'and ultimately in all the principal cities of the world.'

Jessore, a town of 200,000 people in Western Bangladesh, will never be counted among the principal cities of the world. The Army's Founder had almost certainly never heard of it. But there present-day Salvationists carry out a work that is entirely in William Booth's spirit and very close to the heart of God.

Some 285 women prostitutes work in the brothel in Hatkhola Lane in Jessore. Many of them are girls, really. They grow up fast in the brothel in Jessore and become women before they should. Almost 300 women live there – and over 100 children. The women ply their trade from 10 in the morning until late at night. The children just try to be children. They go to school, do their homework, play. The brothel community is ruled by its own laws. The reality is both harsh and tender. The women are both selfish and caring. The place is ugly and beautiful at the same time. It is a place of exploitation and selfless service. All human qualities are present, both good and bad. Everything is expressed very intensely in the brothel. The good is very good, the bad is very bad.

Recently, a new industry has been emerging in the brothel in Hatkhola Lane. Some of the ladies have started to produce candleholders for *Sally Ann*. They make them whilst waiting for the next customer. The design is simple: straw is coloured and then twisted around the base of a small glass. It is perfect for a tea candle. They have sold well in the *Sally Ann* shop in Oslo. Norwegians like to light candles on the dark nights of which there are so many during the long, Nordic winter. The Jessore candleholders take on a special quality. Their little flames reach half-way across the world and bring warmth and light and a flicker of hope to the women living in the shady world of the Hatkhola brothel. They put the extra earnings away in a savings account the Army has opened for them. The account balance rises only very slowly, but with it there is a disproportionate growth of hope that one day they may have enough money to make a fresh start away from the brothel.

Since 1997, Joseph Das has been leading The Salvation Army's work in the Jessore brothel. From a tiny rooftop room directly across the narrow lane, his small team of workers visit the brothel community daily. Trust has been built. Joseph and his team belong. They've seen beyond the surface. They've discovered grace and love in the brothel in Jessore.

Joseph Das is a Catholic with a passionate belief in the Army's social-spiritual ministry. He is a small and unassuming man. Yet he seems to have a giant's heart full of love and faith. He has needed all of his love and all of his faith in his work for the people of the brothel. The beginnings were difficult. The brothel community were weary of NGOs who wanted to come in and spread their particular message. Too many had come. As soon as their funding source ran dry they had all left again. Why should this Salvation Army be any different? It took Joseph and his team years to build up trust. Relationships can only be built over time. There were no measurable results from Joseph's work for a very long time. When one asked about his agenda, he would simply say: to be there. Over time, the team's constant presence won the peoples' trust. 'I Am' said God when Moses asked about his name, revealing that his nature is to be ever present. Joseph's agenda was presence – to be there in God's name. Nothing could better reflect the heart of God.

Constant presence has won Joseph and his team respect. The people of the brothel, funding agencies, government officials: all respect the Army's presence in the brothel of Jessore. In fact, Joseph Das and his workers have become so much a part of the community, that people in Jessore will refer to the brothel in Hatkhola Lane as the Salvation Army brothel. For Joseph, that is a compliment.

You enter through a narrow passage into the courtyard where communal life takes place. Cooking and bathing, hairdressing and ironing, schoolwork and playing. Life goes on as customers come and disappear into one of the small rooms with the lady of their choice. A short time later they cross the courtyard again on the way back to the world outside. No one takes any notice. Life in the courtyard goes on as before. It is a crowded and unpleasant place. Open drains run across it. Used condoms float by. The air is stagnant.

From the passageway some of the girls are calling to men on the street. Their faces are brightly painted much like the Bollywood heroine on the giant billboard outside the local cinema. Their postures are crudely sexual and provocative. There is an exaggerated femininity about them that becomes grotesque, as if they deliberately try to conceal their human-ness underneath a picture of surface beauty and sex. The customers want it. Men flock to Hatkhola Lane. It is reputed to be a good brothel with many young girls. Shopkeepers and office workers, farmers, policemen and soldiers, Indian truck drivers, local politicians. The girls in the brothel know them all and welcome them all for their money. Each girl needs between 10 and 20 customers per day. They keep calling from the narrow passageway in Hatkhola Lane.

Little girls, teenagers, young mothers, middle aged women, old ladies. They live their lives in the brothel. Why are they here? Extreme poverty leads some families to give their young daughters away to a relative who sells them on to the brothel. Working as a prostitute may be the only way to pay off a debt. Some run away from home or an abusive husband in search of freedom – only to be confined to the courtyard in Hatkhola Lane.

A brothel career is often for life. Few ladies leave. They find that the debt can never quite be paid off. It becomes more and more difficult to adjust to life outside. Somehow people can tell who you are and what you have been doing. The stigma sticks. As age leaves a lady increasingly unattractive to the customers, she may take on the role of managing younger girls. The brothel has a well-ordered internal economy. You pay rent for your room, you pay the cook, you pay for protection. Money rules. A steady income is required to survive. The customer is both loathed and loved.

Healthcare was the entry point into the brothel for the Army. A few prostitutes ventured to the Salvation Army's busy clinic in New Town. They never gave their address when registering. There was no need to. Something in their appearance gave them away. Their disease profile spoke volumes. Chlamydia, syphilis, gonorrhoea – every sexually transmitted disease was represented. The Army's medical team were concerned. They saw more than the symptoms. They saw the young women. They saw people with needs that could not be met by medicine alone. Could more be done to help them? It was not easy for the girls to access healthcare. The New Town clinic was far away. Few could afford the time away from the brothel to visit the doctor. It was decided to rent a small room immediately across from the brothel. The help offered from this humble room soon grew beyond the dispensing of medicines. The simple clinic room is the base for an outstanding work.

One may have opinions on the rights and wrongs of prostitution. Indeed, those who can observe a brothel like the one in Jessore up close, very soon form very definite opinions on prostitution. There is nothing good about it. It is morally wrong. It is inhumane for anyone to have to work under the conditions that the ladies in Hatkhola Lane have to endure. But leave the moral opinions at home if you want to work for the good of the prostitutes in Jessore. A moral high ground is no starting point. Instead, occupy common ground. It is only there that you can look other human beings in the eye. It is only there that the arm of friendship can reach out and touch and embrace and help carry a burden. Who is right and who is wrong, anyway?

Dr Mirriam Cepe is a frequent visitor to the brothel in Jessore. Mirriam is based in Manila as the co-ordinator for The Salvation Army's HIV/AIDS and health-related mission teams in the Asia-Pacific region. Mirriam is a facilitator. She does not lead from behind a desk, but by interacting with people, sharing in their lives and walking alongside them on their journeys. She will listen to concerns and worries and stimulate hope.

These inter-regional mission facilitation teams have been a powerful tool for change within The Salvation Army's work around the world. They have focused on the need for the Army to take its lead from people in community and to move its programmes of care and change into the setting of people's lives. As a result we see mission programmes that truly integrate into community life. The Army's presence is in response to a defined community need and the solution is not imposed or provided by an expert, but worked out by the community and the Salvation Army facilitator together. It is a holistic approach to mission, based upon a firm belief in the presence of grace in every situation and in people's capacity for change.

Dr. Ian Campbell, now International Health Services Consultant for The Salvation Army was working as a medical officer at Chikankata Hospital in Zambia in the early days of the AIDS pandemic. Quickly, the hospital was overwhelmed with patients. Every bed was taken by someone suffering from this new disease. It became evident that institutionalised care was not the answer. The fight against the virus had to be taken out into the communities where people became infected. Ian and his teams began to visit the villages around the hospital, caring for patients and talking to others about prevention. They found that people responded to this expression of care in their home environment. Often they found themselves engaged in conversations about entirely different needs from those related to healthcare and HIV/AIDS. People are whole beings. They bring all of themselves into every situation: their emotions and intellect, their social needs and physical needs, their spirituality. The teams from Chikankata found that community-based care was an open door for mission.

Dr Campbell has long since moved on from Chikankata. The world has become his workplace. Everywhere, he has challenged established ways of working. He has brought people from all levels of Salvation Army work together to reflect on mission in the context of community. As a result, we can see a strong move away from institution-based expert help to holistic mission in integration with community. In the process Dr Campbell has become an international resource

on issues related to HIV/AIDS, who makes the Army's voice heard at the highest levels of government and UN bodies.

Dr Mirriam had met Sumitra on her first visit to the brothel. 'I would like to get out of the brothel,' Sumitra had said, 'but what about my family? What are the options? I am the only earning member of my family.' At a later date Mirriam was back and talking with Sumitra again. Sumitra looked at Mirriam: 'You said you would come to my village on your next visit.' Mirriam had not forgotten. 'Let's go – if you can get away, I have the jeep outside.' Sumitra's village is a two-hour ride west, close to the Indian border. It is typical of rural Bangladesh. People live quiet lives in step with the cycles of nature. Sunrise and sunset determine the day's rhythm. There has not been much development over the years. No electricity, no piped water supply, no sewage system. The village connects to the world by a narrow path across the paddy fields. It is a quiet place. There one finds a sense of tranquillity lost in the modern world.

It is also a place of disturbing poverty. Sumitra's family home is a mud hut. Her widowed mother and four younger sisters live there. They are poor, landless people who fight a seemingly endless fight for survival. Sumitra is the only earning member of the family. The money she sends back from the brothel pays for food and allows her sisters to go to school. There is hope for a better future. The circle of poverty may be broken. Sumitra does not like what she is doing. The vision of a better future for her sisters keeps her going.

Dr Mirriam does not pass moral judgment on her friends in the brothel. She has walked alongside them. She knows their reality. Who could possibly condemn a girl like Tanya? She is a beautiful girl. When we met her in the brothel she had only just turned 13.

When she was three, her father had left the family for a new wife. Her mother died soon after. Tanya was put to work for relatives in the village. In return for her two daily meagre meals she kept house and looked after the smaller children. For years she endured the endlessly long hours, enslaved by the narrow boundaries of the life that fate had dictated. At the age of 12 Tanya ran away. She was looking for freedom. She wanted a better life. It was an act of defiant dignity that brought her only despair.

She had ended up in the city. The fast pace of city life was bewildering to her. How could she survive? Who could she trust? The stranger said he would look after her. Tanya followed him through the narrow entrance in Hatkhola Lane. On her first night in the brothel, she was raped and then put to work for her new masters. She found no freedom. The city offered no better life.

Her relatives traced her to the brothel. A deal was struck. Every fortnight they would come from the village and collect part of her earnings. The brothel owners would keep the rest. There would be enough for everyone. Tanya was young. Many men wanted to sleep with her.

When we met her, she smiled and laughed as she was carefully putting on make-up in readiness for the day's work. She playfully snatched the pencil from a small boy who was finishing his homework outside his mother's room. The two children teased each other and tussled for a little while. Then Tanya returned to her make-up. There was not much time for play in her world. She never had a childhood. Now she was growing old much too fast.

The gospel condemns no one. Captain Alfred Mir joined Joseph's team as a volunteer. As Kamal Mir he grew up a Muslim. He converted to Christianity many years ago. Not out of discontent with his religion. But he met Christ and that meeting changed his life. His family struggled with his conversion. His mother had kept in touch throughout, but it was only now, after 20 years, that his brothers would allow him into the family home. After he became a Salvation Army officer, it was alleged that he enticed people to convert by offering them material benefits. Officers from Special Branch Police investigated and kept him under close surveillance. Captain Mir was undeterred. He knew the love of Jesus. All he wanted was to share that love with the people around him.

Christmas was approaching. Captain Alfred prepared to celebrate the Saviour's birth with the people from the brothel. He planned a one-man Christmas service in the brothel courtyard. No Christmas celebration can ever have better reflected the spirit of Christ's life. Alfred Mir read the gospel story. Whores and pimps listened. Customers stood around. They were Christ's kind of crowd. Victims and abusers. They were all exploited in some way and all exploiting others. They were the lost and the sick he had come to seek and find and heal. Like him, they were poor. Captain Mir related the story of Jesus' love. He, who was with God in Heaven, gave it all up to become like us. He who was above all became the servant of all. For most of his congregation, it was the first time they had heard the Christian message. They did not understand it all. But he appealed to them, this Jesus. He understood poverty. He knew what is was like to suffer indignity. He seemed to have had a genuine interest in the people no one else wanted to come near. He had lived a simple life, surrounded by people like them.

When Captain Mir brought out the Christmas cake, they were ready to join in the celebrations. The brothel owner was asked to cut the cake. There were cheers as he did so. Cheers for Jesus whose birthday they celebrated! Cheers for Captain Alfred Mir who cared enough to come and tell them Jesus' story! Cheers for themselves who were important in the eyes of God! Soon the girls were back at work. Life continued as before. But there was a difference. They now knew the meaning of Christmas. God cared enough to seek them out.

Has The Salvation Army's presence in the brothel in Jessore had an impact? Are there any measurable results? Without doubt, there are. The numbers of condoms handed out by the Army team is now counted in the tens of thousands every month. There were only a few hundred being used when worked started. This may seem an unusual measure of success, but it is an important harm reduction measure which helps protect the girls and customers from venereal disease and HIV infection. The brothel is cleaner than it used to be. Many of the brothel children now go to school. There is regular healthcare available. The ladies readily take part in voluntary HIV testing. Some have learned new skills. They have organised themselves into small co-operative production and savings groups. Several produce for *Sally Ann*. Joseph proudly speaks of the ladies he has helped leave the brothel. Their number is growing. It is now over 20. Each one of them has had to make the decision herself. Joseph has visited each one of them in their new home. The Army team continues to monitor their progress and offers help when needed.

Mina Rani Das will tell you that the Army's work in the Hatkhola brothel has brought results. She was a prostitute there for 18 years. As a very young girl she ended up in the brothel as a result of her family's desperate poverty. By the time she met Joseph's team she had progressed to manage three younger girls. She knew the harsh realities of brothel life as well as anyone. Even if she wanted to escape she saw little hope of this ever happening. Life was hard and unjust. Fate had brought her to where she was. She would have to make the best of it for herself.

Mina still works in the brothel. She is there every day. But her role has changed. She is one of Joseph's team. She wears The Salvation Army's blue sari uniform. We enrolled her in front of a thousand people at the Army's 30th anniversary celebrations. She has married and lives away from the brothel.

Something in Joseph's presence made an impression on her. The team's determination to continue their work in the brothel touched her. Captain Mir's gospel message moved her. She met Jesus in the brothel, and he changed her life.

William Booth spoke of 'a glorious harvest' that would be gained when his soldiers would engage in rescuing the thousands of fallen women of his age. That harvest is not yet complete. It is a work that must be repeated in every age and in every place. Mina and the other girls in Hatkhola Lane need that work, and cannot do without it.

Of late, *Sally Ann* has joined in the Founder's campaign. In 1885 he added practical advice to his words of compassion. If the rescue of the women were to succeed, one would need not only a spirit of love and acceptance. Practical steps would need to be taken for 'every girl to be taught a mode of earning a livelihood.' That's the *Sally Ann* way! The candleholders produced in Jessore and sold abroad represent a real hope for many more women to be able to leave the brothel. Sometimes it takes only a tea candle to light up the darkness.

In the slums of
Mirpur, Dhaka.

A Muslim woman revealed to us the essence of practical Christianity. She lived with her family in a slum hut. It was not much of a house, only one room, built from cardboard and tin sheets. It was home to her and her seven children. She looked after her family well and was a leader in the locality. Her husband had long since left her.

The Salvation Army was moving its medical programme out of the nearby clinic into the community. The doctors were seeing the same patients over and over again. They usually presented with the same problems – respiratory tract infections, bowel problems, skin disorders – diseases caused in the main by their poor living conditions. It was time to try to change the cause of the problems. Treating the symptoms would never be enough. Community development issues were added to the agenda. People in the community were getting more involved. Small groups of local residents met regularly with Salvation Army facilitators to discuss both problems and solutions.

We had learned a valuable lesson in a different location. A project proposal was written and submitted to a government donor agency. The scope of the project was wide and the sums in question were substantial. Much care had been given to the preparation of the project document. Surveys had been carried out and numerous discussions held with experts in different fields. We had identified a wide range of issues that needed attention. One that we were concerned with was roofing. People's houses were generally in a bad shape, and especially the roofs. They were of very simple construction, nothing more than woven palm leaves really. A generous sum was included in the budget to provide corrugated tin sheets for roofs that would withstand

the monsoon season. The proposal was accepted by the donor agency and the monies arrived. Things were going well. The project progressed to plan – until the time came for the roof repairs. The community leaders looked bewildered. There was no need for new roof structures. They were perfectly content with their houses and their roofs the way they were. No one wanted a roof that would need expensive repairs in the future. At present, they could gather all the material they needed locally and have a new roof every year. True, it needed renewing on an annual basis, but at least it did not cost them anything. And the structure assured them of a cool house in the hot season. Better to spend the money on something they really needed, like a paved road to the village.

Our experts had to reconsider. An amended proposal was sent to the donor. Money was re-allocated to meet the community's real needs. The true experts on their needs will always be the community members themselves. Development cannot be imposed. Solutions will only be sustainable if they are owned by the people we aim to help. There are too many examples of projects gone wrong. Too much money has been spent on solutions to problems that people do not feel they have.

We saw several hundred pit latrines in one area. The Salvation Army had provided them some years ago to villagers who used the field and the local pond for their toilets. Now the latrines were all used to store firewood. The villagers still went to the field and the pond.

Provided solutions easily become an imposition. Objectively speaking, both the roofs and the latrines were needed. The community had a different and a subjective view. The imposed solution was misplaced effort and money.

It is not only in developing countries that providers have fallen into the 'expert trap'. Everywhere, there are examples of projects and programmes that have been started only to be abandoned without having achieved any significant results. There are too many monuments to expert solutions that had no relevance to people's real needs.

So groups of residents met regularly to discuss both problems and solutions. One such community group gathered in the Muslim woman's one-room house. How many human problems can possibly cram into 10 square metres? We looked around – a seemingly endless catalogue of misery: overcrowded and unhygienic living conditions; unemployment; child labour; all the illnesses typical of poverty; malnourishment; life expectancy under 50 years. The list was long. Every one of the 20 or so people in the room could add their own account of what a life of poverty is like.

Today's topic was the lack of work. Few had a regular income. Most were day labourers. Ninety takas pay for a 12 hour shift carrying bricks and mortar on a building site. Sixty takas if you were a woman or a child. Forty per cent of all people in Bangladesh live on less than one US dollar a day. That is 52 million people. Some 20 of those people were in the room with us.

It was a good meeting. Concerns and hopes were shared. Now it was time to go. 'Can we pray with you?' we asked. There were Hindus and Muslims and Christians in the room. Beyond the difference of religion we shared a longing for God. Faith bound us together. Religion can divide. Faith binds together. Our Muslim hostess looked at us. 'Yes, pray,' she answered, 'but please, do more than that.' There was no guile in her answer. She did not mean to offend. She knew that true religion must touch life. Rabindranath Tagore, the Bengali Nobel Laureate, speaks of a 'religion of humanity, that transcends the boundaries of form and tradition'. In that hut his words took on meaning.

The woman must have been around 40 years of age. She looked old, tired from seven childbirths and from the daily struggle to make life good for her children. Yet her eyes were intense and vivid. They spoke of an intelligent and strong-willed woman. There was dignity in her struggle. What can you do when the world's poor look you in the eye and ask for help? Face to face with the poor, poverty becomes more than statistics. In a country like Bangladesh, 52 million desperately poor people challenge you with their own individual stories of suffering and daily struggle.

You see the ugly face of poverty everywhere. The little boy who has slipped into the arrival area of the airport. He is half naked and begs for money. On the short ride into town there are the countless rickshaw wallahs who pedal their cycle taxis from morning to night. They are thin and tired-looking, worn out from their non-stop marathon in the intense heat and humidity. Outside your house a family of four have pitched their tent on the pavement. All night you can hear the baby crying. She is sick and she is hungry. You stop at the red light. A woman approaches. She is held up by a child. She is grotesquely thin; every bone shows on her naked upper body. You realise that she is only barely kept alive so that she can be useful to someone as a professional beggar. She is there at the same red lights every time you stop. She is there for years. Only barely kept alive to beg. You meet with a community group in the Army's project area. The people are all poor. 'Pray,' they say, 'but, please, do more than that.'

What can we do as Christians when the world's poor ask for help? The Salvation Army has been faced with that question throughout its history. The Army has never shied away from the poor. The organisation has always placed a special focus on the poor of this world. Its traditional response to poverty has been one of provision. Let us supply food, provide shelter, give clothing. The Salvation Army has always been good at charity.

Charity may be noble, but it is no solution to the problems of poverty. Charity may secure immediate survival, but it cannot break the cycle of poverty. If we continue to provide charity to the poor, we have not really listened to their question nor understood their need.

There is a need to rethink the feeding programmes that we operate in the cities of the world. We need to look again at our shelters and drop-in centres. We may be able to sustain the programmes for years. They meet an immediate and real need, but when the funds dry up, the people we have helped are just as hungry and just as homeless and just as poor as they were. Charitable deeds alone are no answer. Charity does not bring people out of poverty.

'Pray, but, please, do more than that.' The answer couldn't possibly be in handouts. A sustainable solution had to be found to help people break the cycle of poverty.

Why were the people in the room poor? The answer is both exceedingly complex and remarkably simple. The complexities are to be found in the historical and political and economical realities of the land and in complicated international relations. Only very complex and long-term processes will be able to address the underlying factors. The Christian Church has a duty to be involved in addressing the wrongs of history and the injustices of the world's economies. We must be involved in shaping the future.

But this would be of no help to the people in the room. They needed an immediate answer – and it needed to be both simple and profound. The answer is obvious. They were poor because they had no money. They could escape poverty only if they were helped to establish a steady source of income. The solution would be sustainable only if it came about through their own initiative and effort.

The Salvation Army in Bangladesh has chosen two ways to address the challenge of poverty. Micro-credit schemes have been put in place. Small loans are made available to people for them to realise approved business plans. This has been very successful. Hundreds of people have been helped to an income. The money has been earned through their own effort, giving a sense of dignity.

The second response to the pressing question of poverty has been the setting up of *Sally Ann*, The Salvation Army's fair-trade company. It is a direct reply to the question asked by the poor in that little room in the slums of Dhaka. *Sally Ann* is about daily bread and human dignity. *Sally Ann* is about practical Christianity. *Sally Ann* is The Salvation Army in mission.

The Letter of James has been called 'the Salvationist's Gospel'. Luther in the 15th century wanted it banned from the canon of Holy Scripture. Booth in the 19th century loved it. Our Muslim hostess in Mirpur could not live without its message: faith without works is dead. In her slum dwelling the words of Jesus' brother James took on meaning. 'Religion that is true and acceptable in the eyes of God, is to visit widows and orphans in their distress.' 'What good is it if someone is hungry or cold, and you say "God bless you" and send them on their way?'

The answer we can give to the world's poor is to live out our Christianity.

"...I gave my
love – and that
will last."

Kohinoor and George had been married for nearly 15 years. Their three sons were their pride and joy. As is typical for Asian parents, their main aim in life was to give their children a good education. They were active members of the local Salvation Army corps; respected Christians in their community. George worked as a driver at The Salvation Army Headquarters. As the boys grew, the money he took home was not quite enough for all their needs. Kohinoor applied for a job at *Sally Ann.*

She was a lovely person with a good sense of humour. She was hardworking and got on well with everyone in her producer group. But she was not very good with her hands. Only too often there was something wrong with the cards she had made. The paper was wasted. She was switched to stitching napkins. It took her longer than anyone else in the group. Occasionally, the seams had to be undone and she would have to start all over again. She was transferred to the finishing department and asked to iron the tablecloths before they were displayed in the shop. This, too, appeared difficult. The iron was either too hot or too cold. The tablecloths were either scorched or crumpled.

Soon, Kohinoor had tried her hand at every possible *Sally Ann* product. It just was not her gifting. She was not good with her hands. No one wanted to let her go, but it appeared that there was no other option. She could not remain if she was unable to produce. It was close to Christmas. Kohinoor was given one last chance to help in the production of advent wreaths. A metal thread frame was wrapped with reeds and then covered with different decorations. Kohinoor picked up a cotton rose and placed it on the wreath she was trying to make. The cot-

ton roses were meant to be used for entirely other purposes than advent wreaths, but Kohinoor picked up another one and added it to her wreath. Soon, she had produced something that no one had seen before. It clearly would not sell as an advent decoration. But it was rather well produced. It was the best Kohinoor had ever made.

Christmas came and went. New Year – and Kohinoor was still working for *Sally Ann*. She now was the sole producer of rose hearts. A metal thread was bent into the shape of a heart and then covered with red cotton-material roses. The customers liked them. Kohinoor could hardly keep up with the demand. She had discovered her gifting: to form the red flower of love into the shape of a heart. Her gifting was love. A few months later Kohinoor fell ill. The doctor at the Salvation Army clinic in Mirpur sent her for further tests at the government hospital. She was admitted. Nothing to worry about, they said. She would soon be out. So she was, but not for long. This time she was taken to the Holy Family Hospital, run by the Red Crescent Society. It was reputed to offer better care than the government hospital. Maybe Kohinoor could be helped here. The best efforts of the doctors and nursing staff only delayed the inevitable. Kohinoor died in hospital after a few weeks of pain and suffering for her and agonising and worry for George and her boys.

The poor of Bangladesh are poor also in death. Kohinoor had been at the hospital for several weeks. Tests had been done and medication had been administered. She had occupied a bed. It all cost money. George was presented with the final bill when he came to collect the body. It represented nearly a year's salary for him. Kohinoor's body would not be released until the bill was settled. Other people might sell their land. George owned no land. Other people might ask their extended family to help. George's family had nothing to contribute. No use going to the loan sharks. They would refuse him money. He was not credit-worthy even to those who delight in exploiting the poor.

We raised the money at Salvation Army Headquarters and the hospital released Kohinoor's body for burial. When we arrived later that afternoon at the Army corps in Mirpur, Kohinoor was laid out in a simple coffin. Friends and neighbours and colleagues from *Sally Ann* crowded the little hall and joined George and his sons in their grief. Outside, the *Sally Ann* pick-up truck waited to take the coffin to Kohinoor's ancestral village in the North of Bangladesh. She would be buried in her father's soil.

People's grief was genuine. Loud wailing and crying accompanied the prayers and hymns. It was time to pay our last respects. The coffin would be transferred to the waiting truck. George and his boys would cram in with the driver and several friends for the eight-hour drive north. As we went up to face the coffin we carried a rose heart in our hands, the last one Kohinoor had made before she was taken ill. The crowd grew silent in reverent prayer. We bowed to Kohinoor, a woman we respected for her lovely personality and her willingness to give her very best for those she loved.

The red rose heart was placed on Kohinoor's chest. It belonged there with her. It was the product of her hands. It spoke of a love that continues beyond the grave.

George came back to Dhaka after a week. He had left his boys in the village. 'I will have to let them go,' he said. 'There are some distant relatives who will take them in. I may be able to keep one with me.' It broke his father's heart, but he knew the harsh realities dictated in a land of poverty. Better for the boys to be looked after by a relative, than to struggle in vain against all the odds in Dhaka.

George did not send his boys away. Sponsorship was found to pay for their school fees. George and his boys moved in with another Salvation Army family and shared their little flat. George continued as a driver. He was transferred to the *Sally Ann* pick-up truck. Every day he takes the same vehicle out that carried his dead wife to her final resting place. He is happy to do that. Kohinoor had found fulfilment working for *Sally Ann*; she had been able to show her heart of love there.

On the wall of a small village church in the north of Bangladesh hangs a rose heart. It had been offered by the hands of a dead woman. She came home to her village to be buried. Her heart of roses says: 'I've left something behind. I gave my love – and that will last.'

Street scene
Dhaka. '40% exist
below the poverty
line.'

The Salvation Army is like the rest of the world: there are the rich and there are the poor. The poor are in the majority. This, of course, reflects world reality. Also, just as is the case in the world, The Salvation Army's rich set the agenda.

From its first days, The Salvation Army's focus has been on the poor. It was inevitable. Its beginnings were in the East End of London, a place of deprivation and desperate poverty. The Industrial Revolution had created a new social class, the urban poor. Political rhetoric was resounding with the language of class war. Socialism was on the rise. The philosophies of Engel and Marx had taken root.

While it is true that the Army would – and will – help anyone, the first call on its assistance came from the poor. The Army's response was a practical-spiritual ministry that aggressively addressed people's real issues. It was Booth's view that moral and physical regeneration must go hand in hand. His call was the social salvation of the world. He and Catherine would not have described themselves as socialists in the political sense of the word. They were people of Scripture. In the Bible they found ample justification to pursue a social mission as a natural extension of their mission to save souls. We may question whether William Booth was a great intellectual, or whether his writings match those of other philosophical and political people of the day, but he was a man of prophetic insights and passionate, practical initiative.

In its early days as 'The Christian Mission', Booth's people operated soup kitchens, shelters for men and refuges for women. Food was sold at affordable prices in Whitechapel. Job creation very

soon became part of this ministry. The poor needed money, and Booth's Army set out to help them get it in the name of Jesus.

In Bangladesh, 40 per cent of a population of 130 million people exist below the poverty line. Behind that statistic are 52 million individuals struggling to afford the next meal; pay for the child's medicine; educate the daughter; repair a broken roof before the monsoon; survive for the full lifespan-expectancy of 56 years. If circumstances in 19th century East London were desperate, circumstances in today's Bangladesh are in equal measure. Booth's recipe for poverty reduction is desperately needed.

There has always been a measure of global awareness and global solidarity within the international Salvation Army. From the beginning, missionary zeal was fervent. Many left all behind and followed the call to far-off lands. On the voyage to India, Western clothing and belongings were thrown overboard. The European missionaries stepped ashore in the Subcontinent as pale copies of indigenous holy men. Young women fearlessly ventured into the African bush. Others willingly set out on their own long march across China. Those who stayed home helped finance the work through the efforts of an annual 'self denial' campaign. Abstaining from some of the luxuries of life for a week could save amazing sums of money. To this day the International Self Denial Fund is the Army's main source of finance for its work in grant-aided territories. It is an impressive achievement to have sustained this fund for more than 130 years. It speaks of commitment to global mission and international solidarity by the Army's individual members.

It is a paradox that the Army has hardly dealt theologically with the question of poverty. With around 70 per cent of its membership living in conditions of poverty, the movement needs to systematically address the ethical questions of rich and poor. A concerted effort is required to establish a 'code of best practice' for poverty eradication programmes. Commitment to the poor may well be in the Army's culture, but it needs to come higher up on the Army's agenda.

Commissioner Paul du Plessis, when International Secretary for South Asia, visited Bangladesh. A visit to the slums of Mirpur once again made clear to us the harsh realities faced by people who live in absolute poverty. The micro-credit project there had also shown that people have the capacity to improve their situations. 'We ought to organise a global poverty conference here in Bangladesh,' he said. 'It is time poverty is placed on the Army's agenda.'

'Voices of Our Global Family', The Salvation Army's first ever international poverty conference was planned for November 2001. The movement's international leaders gave their full support. The General and his second-in-command, the Chief of the Staff, would both be in attendance. Representatives from every Salvation Army territory were invited. The aim was to bring together people from all organisational levels: international policy makers, programme people, entrepreneurs, financial managers – and people with a personal experience of poverty. The voices of the poor must be heard. They must tell us how we can make a significant impact on world poverty.

The Salvationists of Bangladesh proudly set to work on organising the conference. They were proud of their country and proud of the Army's innovative projects, which successfully empower people to find ways out of poverty. *Sally Ann* would be a showpiece at the conference.

Some questioned what could be learned from a conference held in Bangladesh. Our cultures are so different, but the conference was clearly shaping up to become a challenge to existing programmes and lead to a rethink of many long-held assumptions.

Then came 9/11. The attacks in the USA that day were not localised events. They were global both in cause and effect. The world was in shock. People in Bangladesh joined the world's mourners. Many were worried about loved ones who worked in New York. Some had their worst fears confirmed. There was genuine sympathy with the victims of all nationalities. The condolence books at the US embassy were filled with the signatures of thousands of Bangladeshis. The government expressed solidarity with the American people. But underneath the almost unison condemnation of the attacks, there was a silent undercurrent of feeling, a questioning of US foreign policy in the Middle East and whether the US is rich at the expense of the world's poor. These were not just the religious extremists speaking. We heard questions from neighbours and people in the street; from highly placed officials in the foreign office. We heard it from day labourers and lawyers. A suppressed murmur that became audible in the aftermath of the trauma of 9/11.

Western leaders began to speak of a clash of cultures. They claimed to be the representatives of the civilised world. The murmur grew louder. 'The West is turning on Muslims. The war on terror is becoming an attack on the Muslim *ummah*.'

Bangladesh is not a country given to religious extremism. People prefer to give their vote to the moderate parties. But now people became more conscious of their identity as Muslims. When the Americans and their allies attacked Afghanistan in their pursuit of the masterminds of the 9/11 attacks, anti-Western sentiments became more pronounced. Demonstrations were seen on the streets of Dhaka. Voices were raised in anger.

The Army's poverty conference was in doubt. People were nervous about travelling. Concerns were voiced over security at the conference centre. The Americans were heavily committed to relief work at Ground Zero, and the conference in Bangladesh had to be shelved.

It was decided to hold the conference on the Internet. Papers were posted and discussion pages created. Excellent discourses on the cause and effect and theology of poverty were presented. Yet there was something lacking. Although there were some personal accounts of poverty, the majority of the poor had no access to the Internet. Their voices were not heard.

The Salvationists of Bangladesh were disappointed. Especially after 9/11, a global poverty conference in Muslim Bangladesh would have been a powerful signal by The Salvation Army that rich and poor together must seek to address the injustices of the world.

The internet-conference has left the Army with a wealth of theological and ethical essays. They have influenced the thinking of some and there are signs that the questions of poverty are being placed on the Army's international agenda. What the virtual get-together could not do, was to expose people to the ugly reality of poverty as faced by the majority of people around the world. Without such an encounter there can be no real understanding of poverty

The world goes on. There are the rich and there are the poor. The poor are in the majority. How can The Salvation Army be true to its Christian mission when faced with the realities of world poverty? We find the answer in 1 John 3:18, 'Christian love must always be expressed in concrete actions. Words alone are not enough.'

Life on the
water's edge
— water, blessing
and curse.

Sally Ann was never about souvenirs. Dhaka had enough shops that sold indigenous handicrafts. Some were good. Some were bad. Whichever way you look at it there is a limited market for elephants and palm leaf pictures. Early on it was decided that *Sally Ann* would not compete for the limited amount of takas available in the souvenir market.

The boats of Rajapur were the exception. The boats and the elephants of Rajapur, actually. They represent courage and faith of a kind which is rarely seen.

The Salvation Army opened a corps in the little village of Rajapur in Gopalgonj District in 1997. The villagers had heard about the Army from Mr Amiyo Bodiyo who worked as an interpreter at The Salvation Army Training College in Jessore. A delegation came to the district office there to invite the Army to their village.

The community was not unfamiliar with the Christian faith. The Baptist mission had a long and proud history in the region. William Carey of the Baptist Missionary Society landed in Serampore in West Bengal in 1793. His influence on the Bengali educational system can hardly be over-estimated. He translated and printed the Bible in Bengali and published a dictionary of the Bengali Language. Together with colleagues he developed Bengali type-faces for printing. It was said that his son Felix had come to the Rajapur and founded a church there. But that was history. For many years now there had been only very few visits by the priest from the nearest town. Maybe The Salvation Army could provide a pastor? The villagers promised the use of a building, and without further ado an officer-couple was appointed to 'open fire' in Rajapur.

The fire that set Rajapur alight was of a very special kind! It needed to be: it would have to keep burning throughout the worst floods of the century. But first it would have to withstand attacks from people who were very determined to extinguish this 'new religion'.

The village is precariously close to the river. The land is only a few feet above sea level. There were no roads into Rajapur. River boats transported people and goods to and fro. Development had passed Rajapur by. The other side of the river had electricity. The other side of the river had roads – and schools – and a clinic. The other side of the river had moved into the 20th century. But not Rajapur. Here, people lived much like their fathers had lived, and their fathers before them. Farming and fishing, following the cycle of the river.

It was not long before the first Salvation Army soldiers were enrolled. The villagers of Rajapur understood this new doctrine; a God who cared both for their souls and their bodies appealed to them. Rajapur was energised.

Soon a letter arrived at the Army's headquarters in Dhaka. It was from the office of the Baptist Sangha. 'You are occupying our land. Vacate, or face legal action.' Rajapur is Baptist, it was claimed. The Baptist pastor from the nearest town announced weekly services. Religious war broke out. The villagers were up in arms. The Baptist services were boycotted. The following Sunday, two Baptist families from a nearby community came along with the pastor. He had a congregation. Tempers flared. The villagers wanted to use force to prevent any further Baptist interference. Land ownership can be a very divisive issue. It emerged that there was a longstanding and bitter dispute between the Baptist *Sangha* and the village committee of Rajapur regarding the land previously used by the Baptist Church. Any amount of appeals to ecumenism and fraternal coexistence was clearly not going to work. We ordered our troops off the land. Amazingly, they obeyed! A shed of corrugated iron was erected on an empty plot of land. After some negotiating the owner agreed to sell to The Salvation Army.

The corps continued to grow. The officers visited homes, talked with people about their concerns and hopes. Daily prayer meetings and regular worship services were held. The Sunday school soon numbered 500 children.

Then the floods of 1998 hit the region. Floods are an annual occurrence in Bangladesh. The mighty rivers Jamuna, Meghna and Ganges carry more water than all the rivers of Europe combined. Flooding in Bangladesh is rarely associated with rushing water and wild currents. Slowly but surely the water rises until the rivers burst their banks and the rice fields turn into muddy lakes. The flood waters nourish the soil and ensure three crops a year. In the summer of 1998, though, the flooding was worse than ever before that century. About 70 per cent of the land was under water. The water did not subside for three months. An unusual surge of tidal water in the Bay of Bengal prevented the river water from flowing into the sea.

Rajapur was in the worst affected area of the country. Field by field, house by house, the village disappeared. The last house to be flooded was the Salvation Army officers' house. Like everyone else, the officers moved their belongings onto a platform of bamboo which they built at the level of the window sills. Here they lived for three months with the water only inches below.

No amount of water could extinguish the fire that was burning in Rajapur. The Salvation Army corps did not miss one meeting. The Salvationists brought their boats together. In the middle boat the officers would stand up and preach. Salvation Army soldiers were enrolled on every single Sunday during the flood.

Finally the water subsided. The people of Rajapur picked up the pieces and started their lives all over again. Some had nothing left.

We met people there who we will never forget. During the peak of the floods, The Salvation Army provided emergency relief. Officers, employees and volunteers distributed food rations and clean drinking water and also offered medical help. We flew in one day to inspect the ongoing work. Missionary Aviation Fellowship (MAF) let us use their amphibious plane free of charge. Flight plans had to be submitted a week in advance. Civil and military authorities had to give their approval. Anyone could go to Rajapur by road and river. Going by air was seemingly more suspect. Now all formalities were in order. The flight plan had been approved. The corps officers were to mark the landing area with flags. MAF's Swedish pilot had plotted the co-ordinates into the plane's GPS. Even without the help of modern satellite navigation, we could not have missed Rajapur that day.

The extent of the flooding was only too clear from the air. The water stretched endlessly as far as we could see. Only occasionally did embankments form small islands. People had built temporary housing on them, entire villages cramped together, sharing the minimal space with their farm animals and with the many snakes that were seeking out any patch of dry land they could find. Death from snake bite is common during the floods, much more common than death from cholera or drowning.

There was no missing Rajapur. The officers had kept their promise. They had marked the landing area with red, blue and yellow flags, suspended from bamboo poles on a flotilla of small river boats. On the largest boat – a motorised vessel hired for the occasion – our two officers looked like admirals in their resplendent white uniforms. Flying high from the bow was the corps flag. If the Army banner ever flew proudly, it was there!

But even without the flags, we could not have missed Rajapur. It seemed that every person who could move was there. Thousands had turned up. From the village itself, and from every village in the vicinity, people had come to see the plane land. For most of them, it was the first time ever they saw an aeroplane. Few had ever travelled the 50 miles to Borisal where the nearest small airfield is. Word had got around: a Salvation Army plane will arrive and land on the river. From the early morning people had started to arrive. Now they completely covered the two embankments on either side of the main river. The only dry land within miles was awash with people. The number was estimated close to 10,000.

The pilot made a sweep over the submerged village and came in to land. Just before touchdown he pulled the stick back and rose steeply into the sky. He could not land. He had spotted several young men who were swimming towards the middle of the river to be closer to the action. Their dark heads were barely visible in the muddy waters. The Salvation Army flotilla saw what was happening and swung into action. In a well co-ordinated move they closed in on the swimmers and chased them away. Some Salvationists, we noticed, carried long sticks which they used to lash out against those who were less willing to clear the landing strip. It worked. On the second attempt the deHavilland Beaver made a soft touchdown, elegantly turned towards the bank and came to a halt in front of the Salvation Army hall.

In a river boat we visited the people of Rajapur. On a small embankment we saw a husband and wife and their young daughter. They had built a hut of some plastic sheeting. 'Salvation Army Soldiers,' the Captain declared, and we stepped ashore to talk to them. They had lost everything to the flood-water: their house, the fish in the pond, their rice and vegetables. They were left with two ducks – and with a loan in the bank, which they would never be able to repay. The bank would surely take over their land. 'We thank God for His blessings,' the man said. 'He has given us food rations through The Salvation Army.' The Captain told us that they would be picked up by some neighbours with a boat and come to all the meetings of the corps. In desperate times fellowship and prayer become necessities of life. The Salvationists of Rajapur did not miss a single meeting. The floods of the century nourished the fire that was burning in the hearts of the people. The boats of Rajapur. They speak of hope against all hope.

Later, when the water had finally subsided and life returned to normal, a man from the village made the long journey to Dhaka. He had heard about *Sally Ann*. He wanted us to market his products. He made small replicas of the river boats of Rajapur. Souvenirs, really. *Sally Ann* was not about souvenirs. But how could we refuse? They have been selling well. They – and the wooden elephants the man was also making. It seems there is a special blessing on things coming from Rajapur.

In 2004, floods on the scale of the 1998 deluge returned to Bangladesh and to Rajapur. Once again, the water rose slowly until the river burst its banks and turned the rice fields into muddy lakes. Crops have been destroyed and fish have swum out of the ponds. The farmers of Rajapur will have to start all over again.

But this time there is a difference. A new Salvation Army hall has been built in the village. It is on land that has been filled in. It has remained above the floodwater. Even before the official opening could take place (that happened with great festivities after the water receded, with the Baptist pastor of the area attending as a special guest of honour!) the new corps hall was put to use as a relief centre. Salvation Army relief workers from Jessore used the hall for a medical clinic during the day and could bed down there for the night. Food and medicines were stored there and distributed in the surrounding area. The Army compound, rising out of the dirty flood-water, became an island of hope to the villagers of Rajapur, a visible sign of gospel-presence; of Christ sharing the hardships of their lives.

'70% of the land under water... floods are an annual occurence in Bangladesh.'

The 'Salvation Army' toilets in Mirpur.

Leprosy clinic poster

13 MIRPUR: SILK IN THE SLUMS

Politics in South Asia are complex and complicated. Things are rarely as they appear at first sight. Everyday reality is influenced by more lasting qualities like caste and race and religion. History, too, plays a part in determining the present. Very often, the sins of the fathers are visited upon the present generation.

So it is with the Biharis in the slums of Mirpur. More than 200,000 people live in this part of the capital, in what can best be described as a permanent refugee camp. They are Muslims from the Indian state of Bihar. When India and Pakistan became separate states in 1947, the Bihari Muslims fled Hindu India and sought refuge in what became East Pakistan. They are Urdu-speaking people. When the Bengali national movement grew stronger under the fiery inspiration of Sheik Bangabandhu Mujibur Rahman, who was later to become 'the Father of the Nation', the Biharis sided with their Urdu-speaking brothers in Pakistan.

The people of East Pakistan – the people of Bangladesh – suffered increasing humiliation under Pakistani rule. History teaches that injustice and oppression can only last so long. Sooner or later people will rise up and claim their right. In 1971 the time had come for the Bengalis to rise up and throw off the yoke of oppression that ruled their lives. They claimed their land – Bangladesh, 'the land of the Bengalis'. The freedom fighters were brave men and women. They needed to be. The Pakistani army fought the uprising with a fierce brutality that stands out as one of the cruellest wars in modern history. It became apparent that the Bangladeshis could not be held back. The land would be theirs. As a final act of brutality, the Pakistanis murdered thousands of Bengali intellectuals. Lawyers, doctors, professors, poets, artists, musicians: in a short, sharp

slaughter the future nation of Bangladesh was deprived of the best of its educated minds. The nation is still recovering. It takes time to replace a decimated generation.

A later generation of Bangladeshis and Pakistanis have worked together in remarkable ways to overcome the past. The two nations now enjoy the best of relationships, working closely together in the South Asia Association for Regional Co-operation (SAARC) and both playing important roles in the Organisation of Islamic Conferences (OIC).

The Biharis were on the wrong side in the war. As a result they became hugely unpopular. They congregated in camps, hoping soon to be able to migrate to Pakistan. More than 160,000 did, but as it turned out, their Urdu brothers were not too keen to take them in. Pakistan has enough people as it is, and enough social problems to solve. The Biharis in Mirpur and other camps stayed put. They have stayed put now for over 30 years. Every now and then negotiations bet-ween Bangladesh and Pakistan lead to a token few being taken in by Pakistan. But there is no real solution to their plight. They cannot go back to India, where they came from. Pakistan, whom they supported, does not want them. In Bangladesh, where they live, there is now a relatively recent High Court ruling permitting Biharis to take citizenship. In real terms, though, this has done little to improve their lives.

In the meantime the people of the slums of Mirpur get on with life. It is a remarkable place. To the first-time visitor it appears as the epitome of hopelessness. True, the shacks have taken on a semi-permanent appearance, with a good number of brick walls and roofs of corrugated iron sheeting. There are TV aerials almost everywhere, and even the odd satellite dish. The shops are well stocked and trading is brisk. But there are open sewers, unhygienic at the best of times, overflowing and spewing their hazardous waste everywhere during the monsoon season. People live in cramped conditions, often two families – 10 people or more – to a little room of no more than eight square metres. Electricity is poached from the nearest pole. The wires criss-cross the air, often sparking where another extension has been added by simply tying a knot onto the existing wire. There is no mains water supply. There are no private toilets. The public lavatories are mostly in an appalling state with the raw waste seeping through the cracks that become ever bigger in the over-ground septic tanks.

The Salvation Army has a mother-and-child clinic in Mirpur. The work has been ongoing ever since the camps were established. Major Eva den Hartog, a legendary Dutch Salvation Army officer and a nurse, took a mobile clinic into the region to offer medical care to the Bihari refugees. As the camps became more permanent, so did the Army's work. The clinic in Mirpur Section 10 has become a major healthcare provider for the people in the area. The two doctors see an average of 200 patients every day. There is a lab and a pharmacy. The pathology of poverty is all too evident: diarrhoeal diseases, skin disorders, malnutrition, respiratory tract infections. Poor people suffer in ways the rich need not worry about.

Leprosy is a widespread problem. Cramped living conditions and poor hygiene give the *lepra bacillus* an ideal environment. Leprosy Control Workers from the Mirpur Clinic visit the community daily. They teach people how to suspect leprosy and to refer suspected new cases to the clinic. At the clinic, treatment is administered. Leprosy is a curable disease. Sadly, people often come to the clinic when it is too late; nerve endings have been attacked; the patient has become immune to pain; sores have developed and been infected. Mutilations and amputations are only too common. The community-based work of detection and education is very important. Patients who come under proper treatment early recover and no longer pass on the illness to others.

The same can be said about tuberculosis. It is a disease that is on a sharp rise throughout the world. Again it is the poor who suffer most. The Mirpur Clinic works with the WHO to combat TB. A proper follow-up of patients is essential, to ensure that the daily dose of medicine is administered. If not, TB can become resistant to the drugs. The Army workers in Mirpur visit their patients if they fail to show up at the clinic for their daily medication. DOTS – Daily Observed Treatment Shortcourse – is more than an acronym, it is an essential weapon in the fight against this killer disease.

'Can you help us build new lavatories?' A delegation from Section 10 of the Mirpur camps sat opposite The Salvation Army's project manager in Mirpur. 'We are 3,000 people using one block of lavatories. All 14 toilet bowls are broken. There are no doors. We have no water. The septic tank leaks and the roof has collapsed.' The project manager knew they were speaking the truth. They did not exaggerate the situation. The sanitary conditions were appalling, a fact reflected in the records of the diseases profile of the patients who come to the centre every day.

What followed this brief meeting was a lesson in community development principles. There was no denying the need. If ever a community group was justified in asking for and receiving assistance, it was the people living in Section 10 Mirpur. The Army had within its budgets sufficient funds to do something about the problem. Yet the manager and his workers do not believe in handouts. For a strong and lasting solution it was important that the community should be involved. They had identified the problem – now they needed to be involved in the solution. Hard negotiations followed. The Army was willing to provide material and supervision, but on certain conditions: every one of the families involved would have to contribute a sum of money towards a communal fund. They would have to elect a committee and open a bank account. They would have to agree to pay a monthly fee, which would allow for the employment of a maintenance man to clean and look after the facility. The community chairman was not happy. He had seen a white man at the clinic more than once. Surely 'the boss' represented money and could contribute all that was needed. The Salvation Army is an international organisation. They have a nice office across town. Why ask the poor people of Mirpur to contribute?

The chairman's arguments were not unreasonable. It would not have been difficult for the Army to provide whatever was needed for new lavatories to the families in Mirpur. The Army – and other development agencies – have access to funds, and a certain redistribution of wealth around the world can only be seen as desirable. The manager would not give in. He knew better. He knew the value of ownership. The community needed to have a sense that this was their project. They had contributed. They had achieved it. Only then would the project be sustainable. Only then would they look after the lavatories and be able to use them for years to come.

The members of the delegation were quite agitated when they left the Salvation Army office. Reason is a wonderful tool, though. And patience. The project workers visited the community regularly. They listened and they talked – then they listened and talked some more. Soon the community began to see the wisdom in the proposed plan. A community committee was formed, office-bearers elected, a bank account was opened – and then an agreement was signed on legal paper between the Community Committee of Mirpur 10 and The Salvation Army. The lavatories would be renovated as a joint venture.

A festival mood greeted us as we came for the groundbreaking ceremony for the new lavatories in Mirpur. Colourful paper banners decorated the bleak walls of the surrounding huts. Flowers were offered to the visitors. The chairman and the Army staff were served tea and samosas in a nearby shack. Prayers were offered for the Almighty's blessings and the first shovel of soil was moved to great applause.

There were even greater festivities at the opening ceremony a few months later. It seemed that 'all of Mirpur' had turned out. We were garlanded and greeted with elaborate speeches. The new block of toilets – 7 for women and 7 for men – complete with doors, water supply and electric lights, stood out as a building of rare beauty. It wasn't the architecture. It certainly wasn't the surroundings. It must have been the fact that it symbolised a partnership, a coming together of rich and poor on equal terms. We had all contributed our resources. There was no donor and no recipient. We were partners and could look each other in the eye.

The people in Mirpur must be among the poorest in the world. Yet The Salvation Army does no 'charitable' work in Mirpur. People-participation is essential. Anyone – no matter what the economic status or outward circumstances – has the capacity to change and to develop. The extensive micro-credit programme is a prime example of this. In 1976 Professor Muhammad Yunus started the world's first micro-credit programme. His ideas were based on his deep understanding of his poor countrymen and a strong belief that it should be possible to create a prosperous economy for the poor. His programmes have been hugely successful. 'Grameen Bank', which Professor Yunus founded, now has branches in all towns and villages of Bangladesh. It has nearly three million borrowers. His principles are being used all over the world to provide poor people with the means to improve their lives. Even some US cities have 'Grameen-style' micro-credit programmes. Since its inception, Grameen has disbursed loans to the value of 4.2 billion US dollars, with a rate of recovery of 98.90 per cent. They now contribute 1.50 per cent of Bangladesh's GDP.

In Mirpur, people who want to start an income-generating project can get a small loan from the Army. The maximum is 150 US dollars, repayable with 10 per cent interest over a period of 50 weeks. A business plan has to be presented. Two signatories from the community have to serve as guarantors. An agreement will be signed. The scheme has been extremely successful in Mirpur. Hundreds of people have taken loans. Every single one of them has been repaid on time. This in a country where rich people will take loans worth millions of dollars from the banks, with no intention of ever paying back a single cent. The pride and honesty of Bangladesh's poor is heart-warming.

Aqbar had not noticed the small white spots on his skin that gradually became insensitive to pain. He was far too busy eking out a living for himself and his family of five. When he finally came to the Mirpur Clinic and was diagnosed with leprosy it was already too late. His fingers and toes were lost. He could no longer work as he used to. His family slid into deeper and deeper poverty. Aqbar heard about the micro-credit programme. Could this be the way out for him? He could no longer do any manual labour himself. But his children could – and he could manage them and the business. He presented a plan for a production unit for caron board chips. Caron board is a popular game in Bangladesh. He believed there would be a market. 6,000 takas were handed over. Aqbar purchased the necessary equipment and went into production. The family's only room became the factory floor. His sons and daughters became his workers. It couldn't be helped that The Salvation Army's money supported child labour. For the time being the choice was between child labour and child begging, hunger, disease. Aqbar supervised and did the accounting and marketing. The plastic chips sold. There was enough to repay the first instalment on the loan, with some to spare. Aqbar's family business has gone well. He has expanded and now has a small shop that sells sports equipment. The shop space is hardly more than 3 square metres, but both football and badminton and cricket players can get all they need in Aqbar's shop. His children go to school.

There seems to be no end to the inventiveness of the people of Mirpur. A machine to refill disposable ballpoint pens. A mobile canteen on the back of a rickshaw. Recycling of used cardboard. Businesses are springing up and a little income goes a long way to improve people's lives.

Iqbal produces silk in the slums. The most colourful and intricate sari materials in all of Bangladesh are hand-woven in the slums of Mirpur. Six yards of pure beauty. It takes one man a week to finish a sari. The loom is set up and the threads arranged with great skill. The patterns are controlled by punchcards made of cardboard, much like on a piano in the old silent movie theatre, the punchcard goes round and round on a roller and sends the loom through the right

combination of threads to produce the patterns that are so sought after by the women of South Asia for weddings and other fine occasions. It is like a handmade computer. Ingenious.

Iqbal came to the Mirpur Clinic one day with his business plan. He wanted to set up a loom in his little hut, buy the necessary material and produce saris. His is a success story. His saris sold well. He took another loan after repaying the first. He employed one man, then one more. Soon Iqbal had four looms and several people working for him. The *Sally Ann* designers had a look at his materials. Surely they could use the silk to make other products that would sell in the *Sally Ann* Shop? Now Iqbal's silk cushion covers are hot-selling favourites in the West End of Oslo. The silk from Mirpur has been featured in leading glossy interior design magazines.

It is a real-life miracle. Out of the most horrendous circumstances comes great beauty. The silk in the slums speaks of man's capacity to create a better life for himself. Add a few resources and man will turn a hopeless situation around. The silk in the slums expresses the ever-present grace of God.

Iqbal's silk cushions express the ever-present grace of God.

14 HIGH-TECH DEVELOPMENT

The plan was for Sally Ann's IT department to develop software for The Salvation Army worldwide. In the process, we would educate young Bengali men and women and create jobs. We would also save the Army massive amounts of money. Six or seven software developers could be employed in Bangladesh for the cost of one in the West. It did not work out. We could never convince any potential partner that it could be done. People do not associate Bangladesh with computer programming.

The Salvation Army in Bangladesh had already played an important part in the development of computer use within the international Army. In early 1996, the office in Dhaka became the first headquarters to be linked by *Lotus Notes* to International Headquarters in London. IHQ had decided it was time to create a global communications network for the movement. Colonel John Flett was put in charge of the planning. John is a Scotsman, born in the little fishing town of Wick, as far north as one can possibly go on mainland Scotland. Maybe it was because he came from such a remote and isolated community that he chose far away Bangladesh to test out the new system. Maybe he wanted to prove a point. In our movement we are all important.

The few Salvationists in Bangladesh belong just as much as do the larger territories of the USA and Europe. And besides, if the technology could work in Bangladesh, it could work anywhere. We received a phone call late one afternoon. Commissioner John Nelson, the International Secretary for South Asia, was due to fly out to Dhaka the following morning. Could we have a computer ready? If so, he would bring the necessary software to set up the link with London. Anything can be done in Bangladesh.

The technicians worked throughout the night. Before the Commissioner left three days later, history had been made and Bangladesh communicated electronically with IHQ's network in London. By now, all but very few of the Army's 53 territories and commands, spread over 109 countries on all continents, are linked together by an invisible web.

It is important that high-tech development happens in the least developed countries of the world. The basic requirements of the poor for food and health and education cannot be forgotten, of course. High-tech development should never happen at the expense of basic human needs. But it is necessary and important that someone puts high-tech infrastructure in place. If it does not happen, the gap between rich and poor, developed and under-developed will never close. The Government of Bangladesh had understood this and encouraged companies and NGOs to invest in the computer industry, in mobile phone systems, and in other specialised fields. Neighbouring India is a case in point. They struggle with abject poverty for a large section of the population. Yet they have rocket science and nuclear power and are emerging as a world leader in software development. They do it, not mainly for prestige; they do it for development.

The introduction of the *Lotus Notes* link between the Army offices in Dhaka and London was neither very large-scale nor earth-shattering. Outside our little office only very few noticed. It was not very advanced and it still depended on a far-from-perfect phone line. But it signalled a belief that Bangladesh should be part of the modern world. The Army wanted to play its small part in that process. A year later, Mr Stig Sperrevik arrived in Dhaka from Bergen, Norway. Stig is a highly trained computer programmer and a Salvationist. He felt the call of God to give six months service as a volunteer in the Army, somewhere in the third world.

Six months is an awkward length of time for The Salvation Army. It does not quite fit our regulations, which ask people to serve for at least three years. Stig had been turned down by several territories. Mutual friends alerted us by fax that Stig was ready to come if we had a suitable task for him. A brief telephone conversation later it had been agreed that he would come and install a computer network in our newly rented office building. Stig was God-sent.

Quiet and unassuming, he went to work and our computer network was up and running after two months. He turned his attention to training matters and soon discovered that we had several talented people who could be trained in software development. Stig knew the demand for computer programmers in the West and he knew the costs involved to companies to employ such people. Soon the idea was discussed for software developers from Bangladesh to help develop Salvation Army specific software. With training, our people would be able to do it. Technically it was no longer a problem after the introduction of fibre-optic cables had improved the telecommunication links. Financially it would make sense for all.

Stig decided to stay on when his six months were finished. He signed up for two more years. The Salvation Army in Norway backed him financially. The *Sally Ann* Project was taking shape and Stig was put in charge of *Sally Ann* IT Development. A training suite was set up. All our staff received training in computer use. Some were trained as programmers.

We started to discuss the idea internationally, that Bangladesh could work with IHQ and other territories to develop software that was needed by the organisation. Stig lobbied at two international conferences that drew together the Army's IT people from all over the world. We wrote and spoke about it whenever we had the chance. We failed in our attempts. We could never convince anyone that software could just as well be developed in Bangladesh as in London. It may not have been a fair judgment, but to us it seemed that the world was having an attitude problem.

Stig stayed on even longer. In all, he served the Army in Bangladesh for five years. He firmly established the use of computers throughout all levels of the organisation. He spent a year setting up a knitting factory. He gave valuable IT support to the Army in Pakistan, Sri Lanka and India. He trained several persons in computer programming. His final achievement was a stock control programme for the *Sally Ann* Shop. He worked on that with a Bangladeshi colleague. The programme is so good that it is now creating international interest. The Army in other countries may use it.

Stig left for home with his young wife Rumi, a Salvation Army girl whom he met and fell in love with during his final year in Bangladesh. For Stig, volunteering had certainly paid off.

We found the first General Manager for *Sally Ann* Bangladesh at the airport in Bangkok. Well, it was not quite like that – but that is where we met Doug Everett for the first time.

Sally Ann Bangladesh was to become a Limited Company. The lawyers had been working on the documents. The Memorandum and Articles of Association were nearly ready and approved by International Headquarters. The new company would have two shareholders: The General of The Salvation Army would own 99 shares; the Officer Commanding of The Salvation Army Bangladesh would own one share. The need now was for a General Manager.

The first GM for *Sally Ann* Bangladesh would need to have special qualities. He or she needed a background in business management, experience of third world countries and would ideally be a Salvationist, or at least have an understanding of The Salvation Army. We could not offer big pay and large bonuses. It seemed a difficult task to find someone who had all the qualities we needed, and who would be available to come to Bangladesh very soon. But this was our need and we prepared the job-ad, ready to send it out through the Army's network. We would like to have someone in place before we were to leave Bangladesh in a few months' time. The answer arrived before we had the opportunity to ask, in the form of an email from Colonel Ivan Lang in Australia. We can be forgiven for nearly failing to recognise it as the answer to our as yet unspoken request.

Colonel Lang wanted us to know that Mr Doug Everett, a Salvationist from his territory, was planning to take early retirement. Doug was presently the chief finance officer of one of

Australia's largest retail companies with an annual turnover counted in billions of dollars. Doug was eager to help the Army in some finance-related work in developing countries. Would there possibly be a need for him in Bangladesh? We had indeed for some time been looking for a person to help us with a short-term project to re-organise our accounting system. Doug seemed ideal. We sent him an email and before the day was over, he had confirmed his interest to come and help us in the way we needed. He wanted us to communicate more in a few weeks' time. He was about to set out on a backpack tour through Vietnam and Thailand. There would be time to sort out the details when he came back.

The obvious is sometimes easily missed. In God's timing, Colonel Lang's email was not a reply to a previous job-ad. In God's view, Doug was not a finance consultant. He was a General Manager. God was linking need and solution.

It was only later that evening that it dawned on us that we had offered Doug Everett the wrong job. Another email went out. Hopefully it would reach him before he set out on his trip. It did and he replied. The *Sally Ann* concept excited him far more than the finance consultancy had. He would like to find out more. He wished he could have come across to Bangladesh from Bangkok where he would be passing through a week later, but it would not be possible. His schedule would not allow it. He only had a few hours to spare. We decided to ask him for an airport meeting. This seemed like an opportunity that could not be missed. It was worth the cost of a flight to Bangkok.

Doug gladly agreed to meet. A week later he was waiting at Bangkok airport. He looked at the few pictures that had been loaded onto the laptop and absorbed the information we had prepared. Questions were asked and answered. But it was clear that Doug Everett had already made up his mind. The real question had already been answered for him. He was confident that this was God's will. He was to become part of the *Sally Ann* mission.

It was a brief meeting at Bangkok Airport. Doug accepted the post as General Manager for *Sally Ann* Bangladesh. We could catch an earlier flight home, confirmed yet again in our faith that God opens doors that we do not even know exist. Doug and his wife Carolynn arrived in Bangladesh a few months later. Their work has been outstanding. As General Manager, Doug has overseen the incorporation and organisation of *Sally Ann* Bangladesh as an independent company. Profitability has continued to improve. More people have been employed in production. Carolynn has worked as a volunteer for the Army and for *Sally Ann* Bangladesh. Her contributions have been invaluable. God's timing and God's choice were perfect. Doug and Carolynn Everett were God's supply for *Sally Ann*'s need.

That is God's way. If only we could learn the lesson of trust. We worried a little about the need for a person who would ensure the continuation of *Sally Ann* design and the all-important quality control. Several people had been considered, but no one quite seemed to be right.

In her morning prayers May-Britt Lyngroth asked God to give her a purpose for being in Dhaka. There already was a reason for her being there. She accompanied her husband who worked for the Norwegian Embassy. She looked after their daughter. It was not quite enough. She was happy, but she was not fulfilled. She needed to know that she was doing something in response to the poverty that she saw around her every day.

She went to the *Sally Ann* shop that day. She needed to buy fresh cream and wanted to have a look at any new designs that might have arrived. We happened to be there when she entered. Time for a coffee and waffles? Certainly – and a talk. About poverty and purpose. About God's will. Over coffee May-Britt's skills and *Sally Ann*'s needs were brought together – she was employed as a design and quality control consultant.

With her, the *Sally Ann* team was complete. She would work closely with Lily Mondol and Sutu Barua. Lily, a salvationist from Mirpur, was already very ably co-ordinating the different productions groups, making sure that there was a ready supply of the many different products. Sutu, the only Buddhist employee of The Salvation Army in Bangladesh – the Buddhist community is a smaller minority even than the Christians in Bangladesh – looked after the *Sally Ann* shop. She started work for the Army as a receptionist many years ago. Even on the phone, the warmth and friendliness of her personality would come across. When the *Sally Ann* shop opened, it was agreed that she would be the right person to assist the customers. It proved to be the right choice. Customers would come to the shop to experience Sutu's smile, if for nothing else. Now May-Britt was added to the team. God's timing and God's choice were once again perfect. That is his way.

Sally Ann producers and staff from the Dhaka shop — with some of the products.

There are more than
800.000 Rickshaws
in Dhaka alone.

Fair trade is more than a business concept. It is about peoples' lives.

Maria

Maria's father died when she was very young. Her mother remained single and brought up her only daughter as best she could. She was poor, but managed to keep Maria at home until she was old enough to be married off. She was barely 16 when her mother found her a husband. The government discourages early marriage. Together with development agencies they try to motivate parents to send their daughters to school. There are encouraging signs that the policy is successful. Behaviours are changing, but still there are many who prefer the traditional ways. Poverty, too, is a factor in determining how long a girl can remain at home. 'To bring up a girl is to water your neighbour's garden,' an old saying goes. Better to find a suitable husband as soon as possible. So Maria was married off, aged 16. She was luckier than many of her friends. Some left home as young as 12 or 13.

Soon after Maria had her daughter, her husband left her. Again, this is not uncommon. Divorce is possible by law, but very difficult to obtain. It is easier just to leave. There will be no payments to be made, no responsibilities to own up to. The woman is fairly defenceless in these situations. Some special police units have been set up in parts of the country to try and help abandoned women to claim their rights, but they are not very effective. Only a few men are traced and even fewer are ever brought to court. Abandoned, Maria brought up her daughter. Their poverty became ever more acute. Her little girl reached school age but had to stay home. Maria could not afford to send her to school. She barely managed to feed her. School was out of her reach.

Friends introduced Maria to the Salvation Army corps in Mirpur. She soon became a regular at the Friday worship. She found a faith and was enrolled as a Salvation Army soldier. Maria liked to give her testimony on a Friday morning. She was not ashamed to share her problems with the congregation. They were her friends and besides, many of them were poor like her. She spoke and she cried, and somehow it felt good to ask the Lord to carry her burdens.

Maria was introduced to the *Sally Ann* project. Production had only very recently started in a small room at Headquarters. Now they needed more hands to complete an order for Christmas cards from Regent Hall in London. Maria did not know where that was, nor had she ever made a Christmas card before in her life. But she needed work. She left her daughter with some friends and went for her first day at *Sally Ann*. Maria never looked back. Her cards were the best that anyone could make. She is now employed as an instructor and supervisor in a new production group that has been established at the Mirpur Corps. There, under her leadership, ladies from the community produce Christmas cards all year long. Her life does not appear much different. She still lives where she used to live. There are still problems to share with her friends and with the Lord. She still cries on Friday mornings. But she has achieved what was the most important goal for her: her daughter goes to school. Fair trade has made the difference. 'Life is good,' Maria will say. '*Sally Ann* has changed my life. I can now educate my daughter and my health has improved.'

Shathi

In the whole of Dhaka, no one makes better lampshades than Shathi. She will confidently advise the ladies of 'high society' on the choice of material and shape that they need in order to make their embassy homes perfect. She has an eye for it, and hands that can quickly and accurately produce what the customers want. Shathi is married to John Litu Das. They have two daughters. John worked as a security guard. His salary was not enough for the family's needs. He had tried to get better work, but he always lacked the required skills. Shathi could find no work. She stayed at home with the girls. Life was hard for the young family. When Shathi came to work for *Sally*

Ann, things improved. John had encouraged her to apply for a job there. He had been employed at Salvation Army Headquarters. He was still a guard and his pay was still modest. But he had come to know about *Sally Ann* and saw an opportunity for his wife.

The family now had two incomes. It was still not much, but it allowed them to eat better. John had more energy than before. He decided to study. He was intelligent and had enjoyed his few years at school. Poverty had forced him to quit school early in order to work. Now he read social science while on duty at the gate. True, he had to look up every now and again to keep a watchful eye on people coming and going. But he was motivated for study. He had energy. He studied in all his spare time. Within a short time, he had passed his exams and could boast of a Bachelor's degree in social science. It was not long until he was trained to become the manager of the Army's Knitting Factory in Savar, where former sex workers from Old Dhaka were trained to operate commercial knitting machines. Shathi's work for *Sally Ann* made it possible. She says: 'Before, we were always hungry. Now we can eat three good meals every day.' Three good meals have made all the difference for Shathi and her family.

Shefali

Shefali was disabled from birth. Her arms end at her elbows, with three fingers at each elbow. She works in the *Sally Ann* shop in Dhaka, where she confidently helps customers find what they want. She wraps their gifts and takes their money and is known all over Dhaka for her beaming smile. She is also the most skilled seamstress at *Sally Ann* and will complete the most intricate embroideries quicker than anyone else. She was not always that confident. When she came to the *Sally Ann* shop for the first time, she suffered from very low self-esteem. She would hide her arms as best she could under the shawl of her shalwar kameez. She would rather look away than smile when someone talked to her and she was shy and unsure about her abilities.

People with disabilities have difficult lives in Bangladesh. There is still much stigma attached to disability. Especially children with mental disabilities suffer. Families tend to hide them away, hesitant to let others know that one of their family members is different. Superstitions and old beliefs and habits determine this behaviour. Society has not come very far in making life easier for those with special needs. Few disabled children go to school. Planners never consider the needs of people in wheelchairs or the blind. Moving about in the cities and towns of Bangladesh is difficult for the most able-bodied. It is close to impossible for people with disabilities.

The Salvation Army started early to do something for children with disabilities. Village health workers visited every family in their village and found children who rarely left their homes. Blindness and deafness afflict many children in rural areas. They need care. Special classes were started for hearing-impaired children. A home for blind boys offered residential training. Over the years, the quality of this work has improved. Sighted and non-sighted children are now taught in the same classroom. Hearing-impaired children are integrated into the Army's primary schools. Attitudes towards the disabled are slowly changing. The Salvation Army has worked closely with other organisations and government departments, such as Helen Keller International and the Department of Special Education at Dhaka University, to help bring children with disabilities into the mainstream of education and help them to as normal a life as possible. Shefali lived with her sisters. Their parents had died. One sister worked at the Army's clinic in Mirpur. She heard that a new project offered work to women who were good with their hands. She knew no one who was better at embroidery than Shefali. She persuaded her sister to apply. Shefali soon convinced everyone that she was right for the job. Her work is always perfect. Whatever she is asked to do, she will complete quickly and well. Her arms may have turned out a bit shorter than normal. They most certainly are not a disability. Shefali is the most able worker at the *Sally Ann* shop.

Her personality has changed. She has lost her shyness. She is now a confident young woman, sure of her abilities and always ready with a smile. Shefali married not so long ago. She has a son. She continues to work at *Sally Ann* in Dhaka. 'Working there has changed my life,' she says. 'I can now look after myself.'

'... has the Army's mission a meaning for the poor?'

17 THE SALVATION ARMY IN BANGLADESH

The development and growth of *Sally Ann* Bangladesh cannot be seen in isolation from the progress of The Salvation Army in general in the country. *Sally Ann* grew out of existing Salvation Army activities, as a natural response to situations faced by officers and staff of the organisation.

To study the emergence of The Salvation Army in independent Bangladesh is to read a fascinating piece of Church history. It is an unfolding of the working of God in situations that are often very difficult and through people who are mostly very ordinary. It is proof of the sovereignty of the Lord and of his presence even in places and situations where he is not known by name. It is testimony to the almost mystical character of The Salvation Army's essential attribute: the coming together in insoluble unity of the preaching of the Word and the practical service of man in Christ's name. The Army's history in Bangladesh is witness to the Spirit's presence and sovereign working through our service of the outstretched hand in no lesser degree than through the preaching ministry.

The Salvation Army had been working in areas that are now part of Bangladesh since the first half of the 20th century. The legendary Commissioner Frederick Booth-Tucker commenced work with 'the criminal tribes', people who by and large earned their living as thieves. A work-colony was established for their rehabilitation and schooling offered to the children in the hope that they would learn better ways. When the British Raj came to an end and India and Pakistan gained independence, the Army's work ceased in what then became East Pakistan.

In the early 1970s, Bangladeshi nationalists, unhappy with the treatment they received under Pakistani rule, pressed for independence. The resulting armed conflict caused hundreds of thousands of refugees to flee across the border to India. Displaced people filled the camps hurriedly set up by the Indian government. The Salvation Army in India came to offer compassionate and caring help. When the refugees were finally able to return to their free and independent nation of Bangladesh, Salvationist teams from India followed them across the border. People would often return to destroyed villages. There was still a need for help.

A powerful cyclone brought widespread devastation to the new nation. Natural disasters are a recurring phenomenon in Bangladesh, but this storm was particularly destructive. Again, The Salvation Army was there to offer emergency help.

The Army's work changed in character. Mobile medical clinics began to visit the rebuilt villages. Educational programmes started for the children. Advice was offered on irrigation. Practical, hands-on, needs-based work. Many Salvation Army staff were Hindus and Muslims. There was no immediate strategy to establish Christian Church work. The Salvation Army was there because people needed help.

That did not stop the Spirit of Christ from working. His presence is in all the Army's work. He is sovereign. He has decided to stamp his mark of presence on all of the Army. There is no division into 'social' and 'spiritual'. There is only an insoluble unity of the Spirit. That is the mysticism of The Salvation Army; the spiritual nature of the most menial task. It is as it must be, according to the words of Scripture: 'And God placed all things under his feet and appointed him to be head over everything for the church, which is his body, the fullness of him who fills everything in every way' (Ephesians 1:22–23).

The Army's disaster relief and health and development work formed a strong spiritual base from which its first worshipping communities emerged. The strength of The Salvation Army's development in Bangladesh has been the unity of its social-spiritual ministry. Corps have grown from people who were touched by Salvation Army service. The corps, in turn, have involved themselves in service to their communities. That is the way it should be. All of life is worship.

The international Salvation Army's core mission statement says: 'Our mission is to preach the gospel of Jesus Christ and meet human needs in his name without discrimination.' That is a good statement and one that can hardly be improved upon. To describe the work of the Army in Bangladesh one could suggest one amendment that would enhance its meaning: The Salvation Army's mission is to 'event' the gospel of Jesus Christ. Our mission is to make the message of Jesus real to people. That has to happen in the context in which people live their lives. Jesus always met people where they were. He never said to anyone, 'Please, change the circumstances of your life and then I will come and have fellowship with you.'

Bangladesh is in many ways representative of all developing countries. It belongs to the poorest of the world's nations, but Bangladesh is hard at work on its advance. The country has made remarkable progress during its short history. One may look at areas like food production, public health, family planning, education, infrastructure, social organisation and even democracy-building: everywhere one will find that the country is far better off now than when it became an independent nation nearly 35 years ago.

There is a rich cultural heritage that is the source of much pride and much enjoyment. Bengali culture is a living culture, very much part of everyday life in village and city alike.

There are many bright spots in the picture that makes up Bangladesh. But that is not the full picture. There are darker realities to consider: a large percentage of the population lives below the poverty line with a daily calorie intake that is appallingly low. Child mortality and maternal mortality rates are among the world's highest. The physical shape of the land is redefined annually by billions of tons of sediment carried by the floodwaters of the mighty rivers of Jamuna, Padma and Ganges. This, by itself, poses a great environmental challenge, which is made almost incomprehensibly worse by the pressures of population growth. Already the country in the world with the highest non-urban population density (861 people per square kilometre), Bangladesh can look forward to a doubling of the present population by the year 2045. Experts calculate that the population will level out at approximately 250 million people – if the present successes in bringing down fertility rate and population growth rate can be sustained. This brings many challenges and not only to the environment.

There is the economic challenge. How do you develop an economy that will provide work and income for so many people? Traditionally, two thirds of the population are engaged in agriculture, with others earning their living through small-scale industries. They work as traders, rickshaw drivers, casual labourers etc. Only in recent years has the country had some success with export-oriented industries, for example the textile industry that now employs 13 million people, mainly young women.

A distinction is made in Bangladesh between the 'poor' and the 'desperately poor'. The 'poor' are already a step up on the economic ladder. At the present rates of growth in per capita income and inflation, the 'extreme poor', that is those living on less than 4 US dollars per month, would have to wait 23 years or more to rise above the poverty line.

There are the social challenges. Can this male-dominated society cope with the changes now under way? Female garment workers can be seen on the streets of Dhaka in their thousands.

Only a few years ago it was unthinkable for a woman to go out in public in this way. Even in rural areas, socio-economic progress brought about by micro-credit schemes is causing a quiet social revolution. What else can you call it, when the women of The Salvation Army's savings- and loan-groups in Andulia, who never handled money before, have started giving loans to their husbands?

Can the country develop an open and trustworthy public administration? Will people be able to trust in honest institutions of state? Bangladesh – and with her all poor nations of the world – poses pressing challenges to the Church. Does the gospel offer relevant responses to the poverty of Bangladesh? Has the Army's mission a meaning for the poor of the world? It has – if there is no distinction between our social and spiritual service.

At times, it has been difficult for the authorities to understand this strong link between the social and the spiritual. The government controls the expenditure of money brought into the country for relief and development work though the offices of the NGO Affairs Bureau. Every Non-Governmental Organisation has to submit five-year plans for its work and report on the expenditure and the achievement of goals. It is in principle a good and a sensible arrangement, assuring a level of co-ordination and quality control. In a country with over 3,000 registered NGOs it is also a massive undertaking.

For the purposes of its health and development projects, The Salvation Army in Bangladesh is registered with the NGO Affairs Bureau. It has been a good challenge for the Army to have to plan ahead for periods of five years. It has secured consistency at the time of changing leadership. It has also made sure that the status quo has never been accepted as the final destination. New plans have had to be submitted. There has always been a need to show new developments and expansion for the plans to be approved. Financial discipline has been needed to plan five-year budgets.

Relationships with the NGO Affairs Bureau have mostly been cordial and professional. They, like we, are interested in development opportunities for the people of Bangladesh. There have been occasions, however, when the NGO Affairs Bureau has been used to achieve overriding political agendas. The social-spiritual link of the Army has been questioned. Are development budgets being used for conversions? Is the Army pursuing goals other than those stated in the approved project proposals?

On one such occasion, the NGO Affairs Bureau announced an investigation into the activities of The Salvation Army. This is well within their rights of course, and indeed their duty if they suspect that development funds are being misused. The Army's bank accounts were frozen. All counted – officers, employees, *Sally Ann* workers – we had at the time nearly 700 people on the payroll. Ongoing activities demanded a constant cash flow. We were confident that the investigation would soon be completed. We had nothing to hide. There had been strict accounting separation between corps and project expenditure. All the Army's activities were legal.

The investigation dragged on. Weeks passed. It became clear that political motives were dictating events. The situation became difficult. Staff received only part of their salaries. Our clinics could dispense only the most essential of medicines. Development projects received no supplies. No member of staff left. No activity was suspended. There is dedication to the cause and loyalty to the movement. That explains in great part the reason for the Army's growth in Bangladesh in recent years.

It took more than three months for the NGO Bureau investigation to conclude. The very continuation of Army activities in the country was threatened. Foreign governments made representations on behalf of the Army, vouching for the movement's integrity. In the end, suspicions proved to be unfounded. Bank accounts were un-frozen. The lifeblood of money could once again flow. Work would continue.

In recent years, membership in The Salvation Army has increased dramatically. New corps and outposts have opened at a rapid rate, often through the witness of people who have become members when working away from their own community. People are saved and become soldiers or adherent members of the Army. The number of Bangladeshi officers has increased five-fold in the past 10 years. A Training College has been built. Young couples eagerly apply to enter officership training.

Preaching the word of God in Bangladesh is an interesting experience. It often happens that the people who listen have no prior knowledge of the gospel. They may be hearing the stories of Jesus for the first time. It should be noted that in our experience they are never unfamiliar with grace. The Salvation Army in Bangladesh has never advanced where Jesus has not already been. His omnipresence does not depend on his disciples. We take Jesus nowhere. He takes us everywhere. Grace may be expressed in different ways, but it is always present. When the gospel stories are preached they touch familiar cords. People recognise the longings of their heart. They respond to One who makes whole a picture they have seen in fragments. In Jesus they meet a friend who is already present.

Salvation Army history in Bangladesh is full of conversion stories. People discover Jesus and are changed by his Spirit from within. It happens within the reality of their circumstances. Some conversions are ordinary and quiet events, just like people's circumstances are ordinary and quiet. They are proof of God's work, nonetheless. Others are highly unusual and extraordinary. They prove that nothing can bar God's Spirit from working. No circumstance is beyond his control.

Vladimir was in Dhaka Central Jail. He was awaiting sentencing for alleged gold smuggling. He was a Russian and had come to Bangladesh to work for his country's embassy. After some years he left that employment to go into business with a friend. The plan was to import electronic goods to Bangladesh. There was a growing market for televisions and videos, and business promised to pay better than the Russian Foreign Service. Vladimir arrived at the airport's cargo terminal to collect a consignment of goods from Hong Kong. The documents identified the delivery as a consignment of video players. An unusual number of customs officials and police were present. He was asked to open the boxes. They were full of gold bars. Vladimir was arrested and charged with attempted gold smuggling. His friend fled the country. It is impossible to say if Vladimir had been framed or if he was part of the plot. In any case, he was in jail, waiting for years for the judges to decide his fate. His wife and two children could not leave the country. Russian officials were reluctant to take any responsibility for their suspect citizen. Times were desperately difficult.

Dhaka Central Jail is an old and crumbling facility. It cannot cope with the numbers of prisoners who are delivered at its gates every day. It is overcrowded beyond belief. Resources are hopelessly inadequate. But there, too, there are people who seek to do their best to help fellow human beings. One such person was a prison guard who had noticed the Russian prisoner. He wondered if he wanted a book to read. They had only one English book in the prison library. He could get it for Vladimir, if he wanted something to read. He gratefully accepted the offer. He could read English and anything would do to break the monotony of prison life.

The English language book in the Dhaka Central Jail was about General William Booth. How had it ended up there? No one knows the answer. But it was there for a purpose. During the first-time reading of the account of William Booth's life and work, Vladimir met God and became a Christian believer. Later, the pastor of Dhaka International Christian Church was able to visit him and provide him with a Bible. As he learned more about the Christian faith, he started a Bible class in the jail, inviting fellow prisoners to learn about the God who had reached him through the pages of a book. The book was about a man who had long since died, but whose work was still bearing fruit – both inside and outside the prison walls of Dhaka Central Jail.

Vladimir was eventually sentenced to 12 years imprisonment. The day after his sentence was announced, he was pardoned by the President of Bangladesh and deported. He left the country with his family that night, a changed man.

The Spirit of God is at work in Bangladesh. The Salvation Army, like so many Christian churches, is growing. Requests come from all over the country to commence work. People from the north-west, from Dinajpur district, had repeatedly come to Headquarters to ask for Salvation Army officers to be sent to their villages. They had seen for themselves the Army's work in Jessore. They, too, were in need of health and development and spiritual care.

The Army had no presence in Dinajpur. We had no infrastructure in place, no buildings, no housing for officers, no administrative base. It was far from the capital. It would be difficult to offer support to any officers working the area. The people were persistent. Letters arrived with hundreds of signatures, inviting the Army to their village.

It was decided to send two couples to two neighbouring communities. They would be able to support each other. We talked to them. Were they willing to go and pioneer Salvation Army work in the north? Conditions would be simple. Their quarters would be one room. No electricity, no running water, no proper bathroom. They all cried and said yes. They would go wherever God was leading. That was their promise when they were commissioned as Salvation Army officers two years earlier.

We travelled with them to Dinajpur. We were getting close to the villages where our officers would be placed. 'See the village over there,' our guide said. 'We call it "the village of thieves". People there used to be criminals. But that was before, it has all changed now. Only the name remains.'

'Village of thieves' – we were in the area of Frederick Booth Tucker's mission to the criminal tribes. Our minds went back to a meeting with Commissioner Don Smith, a retired Salvation Army officer who had lived much of his life in Asia. As a boy, he lived with his missionary parents in India. Later he served with his Danish wife Solveig in the Subcontinent. Don's first memories were of himself as a very small boy arriving from the boarding school in the Himalayan foothills to visit his parents during the holiday break. They worked with criminals, in an area notorious for its villages where everyone was a thief. Booth Tucker had appointed them in charge of a work-colony where rehabilitation and schooling were offered in the hope that people would change their lives.

Our young officers, who so willingly accepted the challenge to pioneer the work in Dinajpur, would be in old Salvation Army country. The Army's mission had already had an impact in the area. Criminal tribes had changed their ways. Now there would be new challenges – poverty, alcoholism, illiteracy, unemployment. The reality facing the little team of Army workers was harsh. But they would be successful, of that we were sure.

They set about their work in the community. The male officers worked alongside the men in the fields. Their wives visited the village women in their homes. They shared in the joys and hardships of life. We returned a year later to open the first Salvation Army building in Dinajpur. It would not be the centre of Salvation Army work – that would go on in the community as before – but with its white wall and its bright-red cross, it would serve as a visual reminder that here lived followers of Jesus. The people of Dinajpur were once again part of the Army's mission. There are lessons to be learned and challenges to be faced by The Salvation Army from the unfolding *Sally Ann* story. There are the practical outcomes, of course: the experiences gained in establishing a multi-national project; the brand; the business concepts that can be franchised. Those are invaluable lessons and ways should be found to share them and use them widely in the organisation.

Tube well installed by The Salvation Army.

From Fatepur
village.

There are lessons to be learned and challenges to be faced by The Salvation Army from the unfolding *Sally Ann* story. There are the practical outcomes, of course: the experiences gained in establishing a multinational project; the brand; the business concepts that can be franchised. Those are invaluable lessons and ways should be found to share them and use them widely in the organisation.

There are also the more fundamental issues: the questions raised by the encounter with the world's poor; the theological reflections; the challenges to our beliefs and actions as individuals and to The Salvation Army – as well as to the wider Church of which it is a part. The *Sally Ann* story challenges our understanding of poverty. Working in Bangladesh forces the international Army to reply to the question: What will we do about the world's poor? Do we have answers that are relevant?

In seeking an efficient mission in a poor country, we must rid our minds of our pre-conceived understanding of value and power systems. The 'poor' say to us: 'do not judge my worth by my economic status. Do not pretend that you know my quality of life because you know my income level.' We are challenged in our understanding of 'poverty'. Traditionally, our view of poverty has been summed up in the word 'absence' – an absence of things, absence of ideas and knowledge, absence of access (eg to healthcare, credit, education). Logically, the traditional response to poverty has been 'provision' – provision of things, provision of knowledge and education, provision of access.

Poverty has far deeper causes. It is a complex issue and one which prompts sustained debate. But one thing is sure: poverty cannot be eliminated by provision alone. People are poor because they live in disempowering relationships. Dr Bryant Myers of World Vision International spoke of this at The Salvation Army's International Leaders' Conference in Melbourne in March 1998. He concluded with reference to a 'poverty of being' – marred identity – brought about by unjust relationships that cause people to regard poverty as normality.

The greatest thing we bring to mission in an economically poor country like Bangladesh is the liberating news that Jesus has come to give people back their true identity as children of God. By transforming individuals, Jesus wants to transform their relationships and indeed the social structures of whole societies. It is not right to speak of a 'mission to the socially disadvantaged'.

We are not a church that *identifies with* the poor.

We are not a movement *for* the poor.

We *are* the poor.

The Salvation Army in Bangladesh is a church made up of the poor. It is true that we, The Salvation Army, seek the social and economic uplift of poor people. It is true that we do not advocate poverty for its own sake. There is no romance in poverty. But on every poor Salvationist, on every poor Christian, is bestowed infinite dignity by the fact that he/she is accepted by God. We are unconditionally admitted to the fellowship of believers. No minimum income is required. No one asks for possessions or health status: 'Welcome to Jesus, who came to seek and save that which was lost.'

The gospel story is the story of the Incarnation. Someone put it this way: 'God so loved the world that he took a closer look through the eyes of a poor carpenter's son.' Look at where the Incarnation took our Lord. His life began in a crowded stable, progressed through refugee camps and led to a life in tough circumstances. He worked for the downtrodden; defended women who had no rights; empowered the outcasts; cared for the sick and suffering; lived in poverty and died in pain. God chose poverty and he never regretted that choice. He is still on the side of the poor. That fact gives every poor Salvationist of Bangladesh human dignity. They are brothers and sisters in Christ. They are the soldiers God has given the Army as a fighting force to build his kingdom in Bangladesh. The gospel, therefore, is profoundly empowering. Without empowerment of individuals and whole communities, there can be no solution to the question of poverty. The gospel speaks of social responsibility and social justice. No one has a better message to bring than the Christian. No message can deal more deeply with the fundamental causes of poverty, which are rooted in human ignorance, greed, lust for power, selfishness – in evil itself.

The gospel message is also the message of the Resurrection. Christ lives and he lives on through his Church. Wherever his followers live, there should be evident a creative life that manifests the deeds of Christ. Jesus' life of love, his touch of health and healing, his work of deliverance and development must work through us to bring hope where there is no hope, to heal where there is disease, to bring justice where there is unrighteousness, to bring liberty where people are bound, to give food where people hunger. We see Jesus at work when a man in the slums of Dhaka gets a loan of 6,000 takas and establishes a weaving business that now employs 20 people who in turn support more than 200 family members. We see resurrection power at work in the village health worker in Jessore when she visits 300 families every month to monitor the growth of the children and to give advice on matters of nutrition, family planning and health. We know that Jesus is at work when blind boys and sighted children receive education in the same classroom. It is Jesus at work when a former prostitute in Old Dhaka can now earn her money working for *Sally Ann*.

Resurrection power at work through the Church is addressing real problems of real people in hands-on, practical ways. The gospel message is also the message of the cross. 'And he who does not take up his cross and follow after me, is not worthy of me' (Matthew 10:38). The Lord sets the direction for his Church: we are to walk by the way of the cross. The cross represents Christ's obedience to God's good will and his refusal to compromise his stand against all evil. Obedience to principles of honesty and integrity must bring conflict in a land where corruption is a way of life.

Obedience to the call to proclaim Jesus as the only Way, Truth and Life – even if done ever so respectfully – must bring persecution in a land where Christians are a minute minority. Our mission with the socially disadvantaged will only be credible if we are willing to allow an element of protest and challenge to all forces of evil, whatever form they take.

The Salvation Army is faced with some critical questions in its global mission. If our mission is growing in the developing world, are we willing to adopt a truly global view and invest our money where our mission is? We fully recognise and gratefully honour the Christian generosity of The Salvation Army in the Western world. But could more be done?

Does the Army's international agenda reflect the fact that 70 per cent of its members live in poverty? How can we encourage a broader world view among our members and leaders? In this age of globalisation, with its resulting widening gap between the rich and the poor, are we in The Salvation Army willing to speak out against the ever more powerful institutions that control and direct economic policies?

Could we make better use of our unique international organisation to promote poverty reduction measures and fair trade?

Mission is never more meaningful than when it happens in the context of the poor. The Lord wants us to be where he is. If we truly walk with him, we cannot walk on by the socially and economically disadvantaged. If we do, it is proof that we are out of step with Jesus. Our mission with the poor is nothing more than our humble answer to his call: 'Follow me.'

'We *are* the poor.'

Sally Ann shop
in Oslo, Norway

Sally Ann is an unfinished story. The project has come a long way since its small beginnings in Dhaka and Jessore. A failed employment project and an order for six place mats marked the start. A young Canadian hungry for home-cooked crisps provided the name. It was small and it was unpretentious. No one had thought everything through. There were no long-term plans. *Sally Ann* was a response to the poverty of the Army's people in Bangladesh. It was the Army's attempt to be true to its Christian mission when faced with the realities of one of the world's poorest countries. It was a concrete action of Christian love. Its mission was soon defined. It was to fight poverty, to pay fair wages for fair work, provide safe and clean places of work, promote gender equality, give dignity to the workers and to develop their self-esteem. The project also aimed to be self-sustaining in financial terms, thus easing the pressure on limited Salvation Army funds.

The impact on the workers' lives became evident. The project helped them feed and clothe and educate their children. Better nutrition resulted in better health. They could afford better housing. *Sally Ann* became a means for people to escape the vicious circle of poverty.

Sally Ann in Bangladesh is evidence that an approach of 'aid and trade' – assistance given to the initial phases of a process which aims at self-sufficiency – is a sound and sustainable model for development work.

The incorporation of *Sally Ann* Norway and the opening of a *Sally Ann* shop in Oslo – with a second shop to follow shortly – have proved that The Salvation Army can successfully create

new models for international development aid. Again, 'aid and trade' is an apt description of the principles at work. The initial phase does require investment both of capital and man-hours. This is no different from other development aid. The end result, though, is a sustainable partnership that will eventually benefit all partners. There are benefits other than financial: the Army in Norway has gained considerable public praise for its active involvement in fair trade.

The co-operation between *Sally Ann* Bangladesh and Norway is well established. Business principles and routines for ordering of goods and export have been agreed. There is no reason why this bilateral arrangement should not continue for many years to come.

The success of the project thus far has come about through tremendous dedication from individuals both in Bangladesh and Norway. No great idea will materialise into practical results without the willingness to work hard. For most of the people involved, their work for *Sally Ann* has come in addition to other demanding tasks. They deserve our thanks. Salvation Army leadership in both countries have also committed to the idea of *Sally Ann*. Without positive leadership decisions the project could not have been realised.

Sally Ann has greater visions. The view is global: 'Through *Sally Ann*, The Salvation Army will become a global driving force for developing profitable fair trade.' No other organisation is better poised than The Salvation Army to develop a successful Fairtrade operation. This vision emerged very early at the start of co-operation between Bangladesh and Norway. It was shared equally between Salvation Army personnel and business people with long experience from multi-national companies. There was potential for far more than a limited project between the Army in Bangladesh and Norway. Exciting as that may be, it would be a sin of omission if the project ended there. Its full potential is for a global brand of Fairtrade goods, setting new standards in development work. The potential must not be wasted.

This is how the vision is expressed on *Sally Ann* Norway's website:

Sally Ann will be a Salvation Army concept and unit dedicated to developing Fairtrade between developing and industrialised countries. A combination of the knowledge base created in Bangladesh and the various Salvation Army resources and networks, and the position of The Salvation Army in the rest of the world, makes it possible to expand the Sally Ann project considerably in terms of reach and size.

The first step in this enterprise is the opening of a *Sally Ann* shop in the Majorstuen district of Oslo, Norway. Ultimately, *Sally Ann* will become an international network including as many as possible of the 109 countries where The Salvation Army is represented.

Positive steps have been taken to achieve this goal. Through consultations with International Headquarters it has been agreed to work towards the incorporation of a third *Sally Ann* Company. In addition to *Sally Ann* Bangladesh and *Sally Ann* Norway, there will be a *Sally Ann* International, to be set up for the express purpose of co-ordinating future expansion. It will be incorporated in Norway and Mr Jan Størksen has been employed to take this globalisation process forward. Jan was involved from the start in creating the link between Bangladesh and Norway, as the Army's Head of Marketing in that country. *Sally Ann* is a work of love for him.

For *Sally Ann* to succeed globally, a concerted and co-ordinated effort is essential. Salvation Army territories that want to launch Fairtrade projects should not go it alone. New 'stand-alone' partnerships between poor and rich countries are not needed and not advantageous. The *Sally Ann* experience and concept are being offered to the international Army. There exists a pool of knowledge that should be used for the greater good.

Sally Ann has become a brand. Much professional work has gone into developing and launching the brand. It has proved itself to be a strong brand, well able to contend in a competitive market. The qualities of the *Sally Ann* brand must be exploited and protected. Business concepts have been developed that can easily be franchised. The aim is that a *Sally Ann* shop will look pretty much the same anywhere in the world. Global brand recognition is the way to do business – look at Starbucks and McDonalds and Manchester United, to name but three companies whose brand is recognised the world over.

There are encouraging signs that different Salvation Army territories are ready to look at Fairtrade as a way of doing mission. Tanzania already supplies wooden toys to *Sally Ann* Norway. Kenya will supply coffee from its own farm to be sold as Fairtrade coffee in Norway. They also make shirts designed especially for *Sally Ann*, and again marketed through the shops in Oslo. More recently, knitted 'finger dolls' from Peru have become a sales hit in Oslo. They are produced by women from various Salvation Army programmes in that country. The Netherlands Territory has expressed an interest to learn more. The UK Territory has adopted a Fairtrade policy, making it mandatory for its many units in the UK and the Republic of Ireland to use Fairtrade goods whenever possible. Representatives from the UK have visited *Sally Ann* in Bangladesh and Norway.

The Salvation Army in the UK holds a unique place in the 'Army' world as the country of origin of the movement. This is where the unbroken lines can be drawn from the earliest days of The Salvation Army. This is where the ingenuity of the Army's Founder can still be sensed in programmes that have been sustained for more than 130 years. The Hadleigh training farm in Essex is one such scheme. It was commenced under William Booth's direction as part of his employment scheme aimed to bring relief and rehabilitation to the poor. True, its programmes and profile have developed over the years. But its philosophy is still the same: to help people through the medium of work. That is a principle that will never be outdated.

Although by no means the first such Salvation Army venture, the UK Territory of The Salvation Army has in recent years built on this principle in new and exciting projects. 'Mustard Seed' has helped numerous communities and individuals in the developing world to a better life through the provision of micro-credit. 'Seed Corn' goes even further in developing an economy for the poor. 'Seed Corn' is an alternative bank. Loans are provided to Salvation Army territories or groups that wish to commence small business ventures. In addition to repaying the loan, the loan taker pledges to tithe the first year's profit, thus adding to the 'Seed Corn' capital. In this way the recipient of aid becomes a partner in development. 'Seed Corn' is an obvious partner for *Sally Ann International*. It costs money to set up *Sally Ann* production in poor countries. *Sally Ann* has been waiting for a partner like 'Seed Corn'. How fitting, that this should be found in the country of the Army's birth.

The Salvation Army throughout its history has always attempted to be at the forefront of developments in matters of mission. The *Sally Ann* concept offers the Army a practical way to address the question of poverty and in the process to set new standards of fair trade. It is an entry point for mission, a practical expression of Christian care. Nothing could be closer to the heart of Christ.

Special thanks to Major David Dalziel, Literary Editor at the publishing department of The Salvation Army's headquarters in London. I met him in the lift at headquarters one day. Between floors nine and eight he told me I ought to write the Sally Ann story. I had no time to reply. I think he took that as a 'yes', for he started to write to me about this book project as something that was surely going to happen. He has been both encouraging and helpful throughout. David helped me with my English when I trained as a Salvation Army officer in London 27 years ago. He helped me with my English again when I wrote this book.

My thanks also to Lieut. Colonel Ethne Flintoff, the present Officer Commanding of the Army in Bangladesh. She has always been ready with up-to-date information.

'Sally Ann Norway' holds the copyright to the Sally Ann logo. My thanks to Jan Størksen, their General Manager, for generous permission to use this and for all helpful information and comments he has shared.

SPECIAL THANKS

I got to know Knut Bry during a very hectic week's work in Bangladesh. I knew him by reputation as one of the world's great photographers. Now I saw him at work – and I was impressed with him as a human being. He has a gift of communication, making contact with people across the barriers of language and culture. He was unstoppable. From the break of dawn until last light at night – regardless of tropical heat and thunderous downpours – Knut was out there with people. He never let his lenses come between him and the people whose lives he wanted to portray. He got close to their reality and respectfully captured their life the way it is. He is a delightful person and I am grateful that he is allowing us to use his photos in this book.

Thank you to Nina Jernberg, designer at Uniform Norway. She has designed this book not only with much professional skill, but also with much love. She has a real heart for Sally Ann. It shows in her work.